A Primary Teacher's Handbook Music

Dorothy Tipton

Acknowledgements

With thanks to:
Dorothy Mill, Sittingbourne, Kent; Joan Taylor, Crieff, Perthshire; Ann Malpass and the children of Grafton County Primary School, Shropshire; John Ellis; Pamela Stringer: children of Bicton Church of England Primary School, Shropshire and children of William Austin Junior School, Luton.

Photographs:
Heather Grainger: 18; 25; 31
Graeme Simpson: 9; 19–22; 26; 30; 38
John Tipton: 4–6; 8; 14; 16; 28–29; 34; 36; 40
Peter Ryan: 17; 23; 26 (bottom).
Ann Shepherd: 15.

Illustrations:
Susan Hutchison and Peter Fox.

Crown copyright is reproduced with the permission of the Controller of HMSO.

Editor: Hayley Willer   Design: Andy Bailey   Layout artist: Suzanne Ward
Cover design: Andy Bailey/Alison Colver

© 1997 Folens Limited, on behalf of the author.
Every effort has been made to contact copyright holders of material used in this book. If any have been overlooked, we will be pleased to make any necessary arrangements.

First published 1997 by Folens Limited, Dunstable and Dublin.
Folens Limited, Albert House, Apex Business Centre, Boscombe Road, Dunstable, LU5 4RL, England.

ISBN 1 85276 909-2
Printed in Hong Kong through World Print.

Contents

Introduction

The introduction of the National Curriculum music as a foundation subject in September 1992, established a framework for teaching music across the 5–14 age range. This assumed that most primary teachers would teach music.

Music has been regarded as a difficult subject for many primary teachers for a long time, some believing that one needs to be a music specialist to approach the subject confidently. This is not strictly true as long as help is readily available. To date, this has been dealt with by specialists helping colleagues, in their own and in cluster schools, through INSET courses and through literature specifically aimed at the non-specialist music teacher. Much progress has been made and many now recognise that music in Key Stage 1 (KS1) and Key Stage 2 (KS2) can be successfully taught by all teachers.

This book aims to help that progression by bringing together basic information for both the specialist and the non-specialist. It contains 'teacher-friendly' guidance on all aspects of the music curriculum as well as a number of photocopiable resources. A teacher who wants to explore pitch, for example, can find here:

- what the National Curriculum says
- what pitch is
- activities through which to explore pitch
- a plan of how to organise the classroom and instruments
- a basic lesson plan
- suggested music to listen to
- songs to sing
- suggested resources
- a photocopiable guide to pitched instruments.

It is hoped that all teachers who use this guide will experience much enjoyment as they share the pleasure that children can gain from making music.

Aims of the Handbook

This handbook aims to support all teachers in the teaching of music through Key Stage 1 and 2. It brings together information on:

- writing a policy and work scheme
- finding out the meaning of National Curriculum music
- looking at the Programmes of Study
- viewing the progression of skills from Year 1 or Nursery/Reception to Year 6
- discussing classroom practice
- considering assessment
- looking at both exceptional needs and special educational needs
- viewing information technology
- music to sing and listen to
- classroom instruments
- appropriate resources.

Writing a policy statement and scheme of work

The introduction of National Curriculum music means that all schools need to produce a 'whole school policy' for music. The difficult task of formulating this policy and scheme of work is usually the responsibility of the music coordinator, who may be writing policies for the first time.

A dynamic curriculum

The starting point will always be 'Where are we now?' When you think you have arrived at where you wanted to be, you ask the question 'Where are we now?' again and so the cyclical process of development continues. When you think there is nowhere else to go you will stand still!

Where are we now?
Audit: time allocated to music, existing policies, schemes of work, present music curriculum, resources.

Where do we want to be?
To have a clear, concise scheme of work that is regularly reviewed and flexible; to have a policy that allows for continuity, progression, breadth and balance.

How do we know when we have arrived?
Set a date by which you want the policy in place. Governors and parents will have been involved.

How do we get there?
By collaborating with staff; using support where available (eg advisory service and existing literature), by building on and extending resources by having a planned financial allocation.

Elements of a music policy and scheme of work

- A statement of aims (what the school wishes to achieve)
- Objectives (how the school will achieve its aims)
- Content
- Classroom organisation
- Teaching/learning styles
- Differentiation
- Continuity and progression
- Resources
- Assessment
- Review

A scheme of work

A scheme of work is an essential part of the school's responsibility. It is a written guide to the teaching of music. It describes the work that is planned for children in a class or in a group over a certain time period. It will include elements that are special to music and will also show where music can be integrated with other subjects.

Any policy document should see music as part of the life of the whole school. There should be an awareness of choirs, recorder groups, instrumental lessons, bands and music clubs. It is important that the music-making is shared with other classes, friends of the school, and parents.

Helpful headings when writing a scheme of work

Aims and objectives
- What the school would like to achieve and how it will do so.

Content
- The areas to be covered, incorporating the Programmes of Study.
- Topics/themes to be considered.
- Inter-curricular links.

Teaching styles
- The groupings of children (individuals, pairs, small groups, whole class) and their management.
- Classroom organisation.
- The allocation of time.

Differentiation
- Consideration of those with:
  - exceptional skills or special educational skills.

Continuity and progression
- Continuity with previous schemes of work.
- Progression through:
  - skills
  - understanding
  - knowledge.

Resources
- How available materials and instruments will be used.
- Allocation of finances.

Assessment
- Individual.
- Comparative.

Review
- 'Where are we now?'
- 'Where are we going next?'

School year plan

Year group:

Scheme of work	Consider	Comments
Aims	What we aim to achieve	
Objectives	How?	
Content	Programme of Study	
	Topics	
	Cross-curricular	
Teaching styles	Whole group	
	Small group	
	Individual	
Differentiation	Special needs	
Continuity and progression	Recapitulation	
	Reinforcement	
	New material	
Resources	Availability	
	Needs	
	Finance	
Assessment	Individual	
	Comparative	
Review	Where are we now?	

Aims and objectives

Here are two examples, from quite different schools, of teaching aims and objectives. One example is from a small village school and the other is from a large town school. The large town school has a teacher who is the music coordinator and the small village school relies on voluntary help.

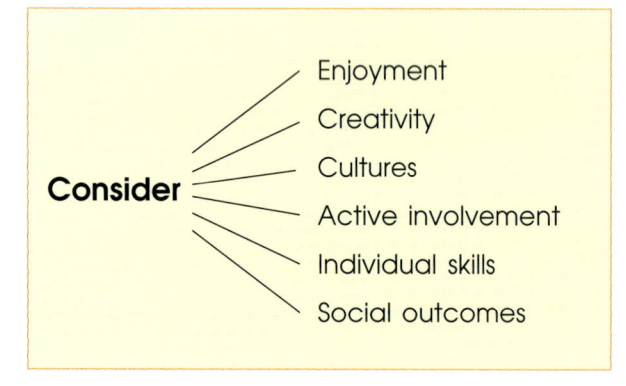

Consider
- Enjoyment
- Creativity
- Cultures
- Active involvement
- Individual skills
- Social outcomes

Large school

Children are given the opportunity to:
- learn how to order sounds and musical patterns
- explore music from their own culture and from other cultures
- understand some of the structures in music
- begin to understand the power of music in different contexts
- explore ways of recording their music using technology and notation
- enjoy music and performing.

The policy document states that:
At KS1 and KS2, music is an important component of the 'arts' side of the National Curriculum. Children are given opportunities as part of cross-curricular themes or as part of specific activities to:
- participate in musical activities: as a whole school, as a whole class, with other schools, with other choirs
- make appropriate use of information technology to create and record music.

Small school

Children are given the opportunity to:
- enjoy music that they create themselves
- appreciate a variety of styles of music
- develop understanding and knowledge of music through making and listening to music, enabling them to work at their own appropriate level and to refine their own skills.

The policy document states that:
- music is largely a practical activity
- all children should have access to instrument lessons and singing lessons
- all children should have access to recorded music.

Organising content

There are a variety of ways in which the content can be organised so that all the requirements of the National Curriculum music can be achieved. Each school will find the most appropriate to its own situation.

The sample schools have taken two quite different approaches. The small school has given its non-specialist staff a broad plan from which to choose activities. This lends itself to integration with project work and still covers the requirements of KS1 and KS2.

The larger school has more specific plans, a situation where

more teachers might need guidance. A termly/yearly plan, based on the Programmes of Study, is presented by a specialist.

Small school

Creative music
From the beginning of KS1 developing through to KS2 the children are to be involved in the following activities:
- exploring sounds – playing a range of percussion instruments
- learning to play in a group with others – expressing their feelings through music
- telling stories illustrated with music
- memorising simple rhymes to repeat and to teach others
- learning to play a recorder (voluntary)
- recording in simple form, using symbols and developing recognised music notation
- using creative dance to interpret their feelings.

Singing
The children sing:
- in a whole school or class situation
- rhymes, action songs and popular songs.

Listening and performing
The children listen to and perform:
- music from different periods and cultures.

Large school

Autumn term

Year 3
The children:
- use music cards (County Project) to explore sounds
- learn the correct names for instruments
- learn how to use the instruments
- play rhythm games: 'Clapping Names', 'Pass the Rhythm'
- listen to music about animals.

Year 4
The children:
- take the rhythm of a nursery rhyme or a sentence and create a tune, using a pentatonic scale
- develop rhythm work – using football teams
- are introduced to the terms: bar, crotchet and quaver
- make flashcards
- play rhythm games
- listen to music about storms.

Music in the National Curriculum

Attainment Targets
Performing and composing

Key Stage 1

The children should demonstrate their ability to:

- 🖐 sing a variety of songs
- 🖐 play simple pieces
- 🖐 play accompaniments with confidence
- 🖐 play with an awareness of pulse
- 🖐 explore, select and order sounds
- 🖐 make compositions with simple structures
- 🖐 make expressive use of some sounds.

The children should:

- 🖐 be introduced to a wide range of unison songs (eg rhymes and action songs)
- 🖐 use tuned instruments to discover and memorise easy, well-known tunes
- 🖐 use untuned instruments (tambourine, triangle, drum, wood block) to play repetitive accompaniments
- 🖐 listen to, and be aware of, the beat/pulse of a piece (eg waltz, march, lullaby)
- 🖐 experiment with a variety of instruments, and with voice and body percussion
- 🖐 place sounds in an acceptable order (eg create a beginning, middle and end)
- 🖐 use sounds in a creative way, using pitch, duration and tempo to create musical effects (eg a walk by the sea).

Key Stage 2

The children should demonstrate their ability to:

- 🖐 perform accurately and confidently
- 🖐 make expressive use of musical elements
- 🖐 show an awareness of phrase
- 🖐 sing songs and rounds that have two parts
- 🖐 maintain independent instrumental lines with an awareness of other performers
- 🖐 select and combine appropriate resources
- 🖐 use musical structures
- 🖐 make expressive use of musical elements in an organised way
- 🖐 use symbols when performing/ communicating musical ideas.

The children should:

- 🖐 take more care to play and sing that which is written by the composer
- 🖐 become aware of volume, speed and length of notes
- 🖐 shape a phrase by breathing at the end of it
- 🖐 develop a wider repertoire of rounds and songs
- 🖐 play a different tune from that of a partner or the rest of the class while being conscious of the sound and effect created
- 🖐 experiment with, and combine appropriately, the sounds of a variety of instruments
- 🖐 create music to set patterns – repeat tunes (ostinato) and add a chorus
- 🖐 create atmosphere by using volumes and speeds, in an organised way
- 🖐 use either graphic or traditional notation for playing and singing.

Attainment Targets
Listening and appraising

Key Stage 1

The children should demonstrate their ability to:

✋ respond to short pieces of music

✋ recognise repetition and changes within the musical elements

✋ listen attentively
✋ describe sounds

✋ compare sounds and pieces of music using simple terms.

The children should:

✋ listen and respond to music, through movement, dance, art or any other form of expression
✋ listen for any obvious examples of repeated tunes and rhythms, and be aware of/ discuss any changes in dynamics, pitch, length, timbre
✋ be active only as a listener
✋ be able to describe and make comments on sounds (including everyday sounds)
✋ use a musical vocabulary to describe pieces of music which should include the elements: pitch, duration, timbre, dynamics, texture and classroom instrument names.

Key Stage 2

The children should demonstrate their ability to:

✋ respond to music, identifying changes in character and mood
✋ recognise how musical elements and resources are used to communicate moods and ideas

✋ evaluate their own work and identify how it can be improved

✋ begin to recognise how music is affected by time and place, including the intentions of composer and performer

✋ listen with attention to detail and describe music from different traditions using a music vocabulary.

The children should:

✋ listen to music, noticing any significant changes and discussing them
✋ be aware of how dynamics, pitch, rhythms, voices and instruments can be used to create moods and communicate ideas
✋ listen to their own and other people's music compositions, making constructive comments and suggesting improvements
✋ listen to music from different countries and times, finding similarities and differences (instruments available, typical rhythmic patterns) and discovering what the composer and performer are intending to communicate
✋ listen carefully and discuss all music using appropriate language.

Key Stage

1

Programmes of Study
Performing and composing

WHAT IT SAYS	KEY IDEAS	WHAT IT MEANS
A Sing songs from memory, developing control of breathing, dynamics, rhythm and pitch.	**VOICE CONTROL** **AWARENESS OF MUSICAL ELEMENTS**	Control the sounds made by the voice when singing a variety of songs. Be aware of the musical elements – loud/soft, high/low.
B Play simple pieces and accompaniments, and perform short musical patterns by ear and from symbols.	**INSTRUMENTAL CONTROL** **MUSICAL PATTERNS** **SIMPLE NOTATION**	Control the sounds made by a range of tuned/untuned percussion instruments in simple pieces and perform musical patterns (repeated notes) by listening to music and by following simple notation (graphics).
C Sing and play unison pieces to develop an awareness of other performers.	**REHEARSE AND PERFORM**	Perform with others, becoming aware of audience, venue and occasion (classroom/school/concert).
D Rehearse and share music-making.	**SHARE/ AUDIENCE**	Work together in groups and share the pleasure of making music.
E Improvise musical patterns (eg invent and change patterns whilst playing and singing).	**IMPROVISE** **CHANGE PATTERNS**	Experiment, discover and create new musical patterns while in the process of playing and singing.
F Explore, create, select and organise sounds in simple structures.	**EXPLORE, SELECT AND ORGANISE SOUNDS** **SIMPLE STRUCTURES**	Explore a range of sound resources – voices, instruments, environmental sounds – and use them in a structured way to compose a piece of music.
G Use sounds to create musical effects (eg to suggest a machine or a walk through a forest).	**COMMUNICATE EFFECTS**	Communicate musical effects to an audience using elements such as dynamics (loud/soft), timbre (rattling/tinkling/smooth), tempo (fast/slow).
H Record the children's compositions using symbols, where appropriate.	**RECORD/RETAIN** **GRAPHIC SYMBOLS**	Invent graphic symbols to record pieces of composition.

Key Stage 2

Programmes of Study
Performing and composing

WHAT IT SAYS	KEY IDEAS	WHAT IT MEANS
A Sing songs, developing control of diction and musical elements, particularly phrasing (eg giving shape to a song by breathing at the end of a phrase).	**CONTROL OF DICTION AND BREATHING**	Sing a wide variety of songs, taking care with the clarity of words as well as the rhythm, speed, dynamics and pitch. The children should be taught to breathe at the end of a phrase.
B Play pieces and accompaniments, and perform musical patterns by ear and from notations (eg symbols that define musical elements) with increasing dexterity and control.	**PLAY BY EAR** **MUSICAL PATTERNS**	Listen to, experiment with, and play from memory, pieces and accompaniments. Experiment with musical patterns (eg repeated tunes, 'Questions and Answers', 'Echoes'). Create a simple graphic score showing: duration, dynamics, speed.
C Sing songs and play pieces that have two or more parts to develop the ability to listen to other performers.	**PART SING**	Extend song and playing repertoire into rounds and part songs/pieces, being aware of other performers.
D Rehearse and present projects and performances.	**ORGANISE REHEARSALS**	Organise a rehearsal schedule and performance.
E Improvise rhythmic and melodic ideas (eg add a percussion part to a song).	**IMPROVISE**	Experiment on different instruments (tuned and untuned) with rhythms and tunes, to find a suitable accompaniment.
F Explore, create, select, combine and organise sounds in musical structures, (eg using repeated sections or a structure with verses and a chorus).	**USE MUSICAL STRUCTURES**	Experiment with a variety of sounds (including voices, instruments, environmental sounds) and place them in musical patterns – binary AB/ternary ABA/ rondo ABACADA.
G Use sounds and structures to achieve an intended effect (eg to create a particular atmosphere where appropriate).	**CREATE AN ATMOSPHERE**	Use sounds (sliding, gliding, shaking, jumping, heavy, light, long, short) and structures to describe an atmosphere (eg sunset over the sea).
H Refine and record compositions, using notation where appropriate.	**REFINE** **RECORD** **NOTATE**	Listen to, discuss, alter, replay, record compositions and use appropriate notation (graphic/traditional) to record results.

Key Stage 1

Programmes of Study
Listening and appraising

WHAT IT SAYS	KEY IDEAS	WHAT IT MEANS
A Recognise how sounds can be made in different ways (eg by blowing, plucking, shaking, vocalising).	**SOUNDS MADE IN A VARIETY OF WAYS**	Experiment with a wide variety of instruments, found objects and voices, to see how many different kinds of sounds can be created. Discuss the differences.
B Recognise how sounds are used in music to achieve particular effects (eg to soothe, to excite).	**SOUNDS FOR PARTICULAR EFFECTS**	Listen to special kinds of music – lullaby, rain dance, war march, lament, and discuss how the effects are achieved.
C Recognise that music comes from different times and places.	**MUSIC FROM OTHER TIMES AND PLACES**	Listen to music from different times (eg early church music/twentieth century pop music) and from different places (eg Africa, Spain, Scotland) and discuss how it takes the character of the time/place.
D Respond to musical elements and the changing character and moods of a piece of music by means of dance and other suitable forms of expression.	**RESPONSE TO MUSIC THROUGH DANCE**	Listen and respond to the mood of a piece of music through dance, movement, art, craft, poetry or any other expressive form.
E Describe, in simple terms, the sounds that are listened to, performed, composed or heard, including everyday sounds.	**MUSIC VOCABULARY**	Build up a musical vocabulary to enable the children to describe their own, and other people's, music and performances, as well as the sounds of the environment.

A PRIMARY TEACHER'S HANDBOOK – *Music*

Key Stage 2

WHAT IT SAYS	KEY IDEAS	WHAT IT MEANS
A Identify the sounds made by a variety of instruments individually and in combination (eg classroom instruments and families of instruments).	**IDENTIFY INSTRUMENT SOUNDS**	Listen to and identify the distinct sounds made by one instrument or those in a small group, eg (1) xylophone (2) drum, tambourine/triangle (3) violin (4) flute, clarinet, bassoon.
B Identify how musical elements and resources (eg voices, instruments, performers) can be used to communicate a mood or effect.	**MOODS AND EFFECTS**	Listen to a piece of music that communicates a special mood and discuss how this effect has been created (eg the music gets gradually louder or softer, there are a variety of instrumental sounds, tunes are used that weave into one another).
C Recognise ways in which music reflects the time and place in which it is created.	**TIME AND PLACE**	Listen to music from other times and places and discuss why it takes on its special character (eg calypso, samba, African drums).
D Compare music from contrasting musical traditions and respond to differences in character and mood (eg through dance or other suitable forms of expression).	**MUSICAL TRADITIONS**	Listen to music from the European 'classical' tradition, from other cultures across the world, from the regions of the British Isles and to folk and popular music. Compare these and respond to them through dance, art or poetry.
E Express ideas and opinions about music, developing a musical vocabulary and the ability to use musical knowledge to support views.	**MUSICAL KNOWLEDGE** **EXTENDED VOCABULARY**	Develop an independent view of music – an expression of likes and dislikes that is based on musical knowledge. These opinions should be expressed through an acquired musical vocabulary.

A PRIMARY TEACHER'S HANDBOOK – *Music*

Progression through skills

Performing

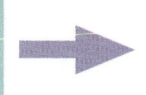
Sings songs from memory, developing control of breathing, dynamics, rhythm, pitch.

Nursery/Reception

Uses the voice as a sound-making instrument, and experiments with sounds.

Plays simple pieces and accompaniments.

Performs short musical patterns by ear and from symbols.

Becomes more aware of other performers and players.

Becomes more aware of other people in a group and the sounds created.

Plays pieces that have several parts.

Develops a greater awareness of an audience, venue, occasion.

Rehearses and presents own projects/performances.

Develops a repertoire of two-part songs and rounds.

Year 6

Performs musical patterns by ear and from notation.

Sings songs, making greater use of breath control, phrasing, diction.

A PRIMARY TEACHER'S HANDBOOK – *Music*

𝒫erforming

SKILLS	SUGGESTED ACTIVITIES
✋ Singing songs from memory, developing control of: breathing, dynamics, rhythm, pitch.	✋ Use action songs, nursery rhymes, counting, topic-linked songs, playground singing games and festival-linked songs.
✋ Using the voice as a sound-making instrument.	✋ Pass a vocal sound around a circle (high/low/low to high/short/long/loud to soft/re-created environmental sounds).
✋ Playing simple pieces and accompaniments.	✋ Use a drone (a single note), an ostinato (a short repeated tune) or a steady pulse on untuned percussion instruments to accompany a song.
✋ Performing short musical patterns by ear and from symbols.	✋ Break down simple tunes into short sections. Learn these short sections from memory and then put them together again. Create easy-to-understand symbols and play some of these to each other.
✋ Becoming more aware of other performers and players.	✋ Be aware of one another by deciding: 'Where do we sit?' 'Can we see the conductor?' Listen and wait. Encourage silence at the beginning and at the end of a performance.
✋ Developing a greater awareness of an audience, venue, occasion.	✋ Play to one another, to other classes, in an assembly, for a special occasion.
✋ Singing songs, making greater use of breath control, phrasing, diction.	✋ Look at the phrases in a song – encourage breathing at the end, practise controlled breathing, sing tongue twisters to help diction, sing quietly as well as loudly.
✋ Performing musical patterns by ear and from notation.	✋ Listen to a simple musical pattern and try to copy it. In pairs, play five notes (CDEGA) on an instrument, play echoes, write down notation for a partner to play.
✋ Developing a repertoire of two-part songs and rounds.	✋ Sing rounds, canons, part songs, descants.
✋ Playing pieces that have several parts.	✋ Find some simple tunes with parts and use recorder players, instrumentalists and voices for these parts.
✋ Becoming more aware of other people in a group.	✋ Listen carefully to others for timing, tuning, timbre; help younger children with their performances.
✋ Rehearsing and presenting own projects/performances.	✋ Decide the best position for each instrument in the group/orchestra (consider sound and vision). Set up electronic instruments with help and perform to other classes or schools.

Composing

Creates simple musical sequences, plays 'Simon Says', 'Name Clapping', 'Questions and Answers',

Nursery/Reception

Explores sounds in the environment.

Explores vocal, body and instrumental sounds (tuned/untuned percussion); explores high/low, short/long, fast/slow. Creates symbols to represent these.

Makes sound pictures using all the appropriate elements (dynamics, pitch, duration); responds to poetry and art.

Improvises musical patterns (changes patterns while playing/singing songs or nursery rhymes).

Tiger in a Tropical Storm The work of Henri Rousseau was used as a stimulus for collaborative Art, Poetry and Music which was shared with a wider audience at the West Midlands Show. Would you like to share our composition and performance with us? Please use the tape recorder.

Explores, creates, selects and organises sounds into simple structures (eg using drones, ostinato, pentatonic scale).

Uses sounds and structures to achieve an intended effect – an appropriate piece for a festival.

Explores, creates, selects and organises sounds in musical structures – uses verses and chorus, and rondo form (ABACA).

Uses sounds to portray a story using vocal/instrumental/acoustic/electronic sounds to describe events/characters.

Uses notation to refine and record compositions.

Improvises in different styles, creates new musical patterns while singing or playing.

Devises ways to write down sounds – graphic notation.

Year 6

Composing

SKILLS	SUGGESTED ACTIVITIES
✋ Exploring sounds in the environment.	✋ Listen to, recognise, and use sounds from: the classroom, school, countryside, home, town. Record and re-create these.
✋ Exploring vocal, body and instrumental sounds.	✋ Play 'Hunt the Thimble' using dynamics – discover sliding, jumping and hopping sounds. Use the voice in high/low echoes.
✋ Creating simple musical patterns.	✋ Play 'Simon Says' using musical patterns, clapping, clicking, knee slapping. Pass sounds around a circle. Play 'Name Clapping'.
✋ Making sound pictures.	✋ Decide on a picture to be created. Choose a group of instruments (eg wood, metal). Create appropriate sounds. Build up the picture, sound on sound.
✋ Improvising musical patterns.	✋ Agree on a rhythmic word phrase chosen by a pupil (eg 'good morning'). How can it be changed (short, long)? Try to combine a few of the variations.
✋ Organising sounds into simple structures.	✋ Introduce the idea of repetition using a sandwich structure (ABA). Contrast high and low sounds, and hard and soft sounds to create simple pieces.
✋ Using sounds to portray a story.	✋ Choose the speed, dynamics and duration of appropriate sounds to portray a given story or painting.
✋ Devising ways to write down sounds.	✋ Hear a sound (eg tambourine shaking) and discuss how it could be written down. Explore many instrumental sounds in this way.
✋ Improvising while playing/singing.	✋ Improvise vocally on a simple piece using two notes only. Create an accompaniment (on untuned percussion) for a known song while playing/singing.
✋ Organising sounds in musical structures.	✋ Discuss rondo form, where a tune reoccurs (ABACA). Create short pieces and join these together to create a school rondo, a fairground rondo and a machine rondo.
✋ Using sounds and structures to achieve an intended effect.	✋ Compose short pieces of music to celebrate festivals (eg Christmas, Harvest, birthdays, Chinese New Year, African rain dance, Indian Divali).
✋ Using notation to refine and record compositions.	✋ Discuss and encourage the use of: graphic notation, western staff notation and written instructions.

Listening

Nursery/Reception

Listens to and recognises the sounds of the classroom (high/low/soft/hard/short/long).

Listens to and recognises sounds of the school and local environment – some getting louder, some getting softer, contrasting: short and long, high and low, sound and silence.

Recognises how sounds are made vocally and through using body percussion (clicking fingers, tapping toes, clapping hands).

Recognises how sounds are made on different instruments by blowing, plucking, shaking, tapping, stroking.

Recognises how sound can be used to create an effect (eg to soothe, to excite, to create a frightening atmosphere).

INSTRUMENTS TO

SCRAPE

TAP/HIT

Can you think of an instrument you could PLUCK?

SHAKE

BLOW

Listens to music from different places – Scotland, Ireland, Wales, Europe, Africa and so on.

Identifies how the elements of music are used to communicate mood or effect – by instruments.

Identifies how the elements of music are used to communicate mood or effect – by voice.

Recognises how music reflects the age in which it is written and how music takes on the character of the place.

Recognises the sound of a family of instruments – percussion and orchestral.

Listens to music from different times – from early church music to modern pop.

Year 6

Recognises the individual sounds of instruments – percussion and orchestral.

A PRIMARY TEACHER'S HANDBOOK – *Music*

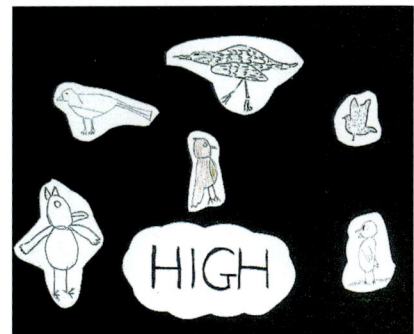

Listening

SKILLS	SUGGESTED ACTIVITIES
Listening to and recognising the sounds of the classroom.	Ask the children to close their eyes and identify everyday sounds – door banging, tap dripping, each other's voices. Which sounds are high/low/long/short/loud/soft?
Listening to and recognising the sounds of the school and local environment.	Listen to footsteps getting nearer/further away. Notice the changes in sounds of an aeroplane, a fire engine, a police car, a kettle boiling.
Recognising how sounds are made vocally and through body percussion.	Vocally – respond to a wavy line, making voice go high/low. Body percussion – respond to and recognise the sound of silence when clapping, clicking.
Recognising how sounds are made on different instruments.	Demonstrate – blowing, plucking, shaking, tapping instruments. How do you do it? What is happening to the instrument?
Recognising how sounds can be used to create an effect.	Listen to a calm piece of music in the middle of chaos or on a windy day. Respond through dance and drama to lively music.
Listening to music from different places.	Introduce the children to a collection of instruments from other countries. Listen to and discuss music from Africa, Spain, Scotland. Respond using castanets, drums, pipes.
Listening to music from different times.	Play two pieces of music – early church music and current music. Is there any difference? Which do the children prefer? (Discuss acoustic and electronic sounds.)
Recognising the individual sounds of instruments.	Divide the classroom percussion instruments into groups of wood, metal, skin or hitting and shaking. Can one child, when blindfolded, recognise which group plays?
Recognising the sound of a family of instruments.	Behind a screen play a single instrument. What is it? Listen to recorded music of single orchestral instruments and discuss their sounds. How are they made?
Identifying how the elements of music are used to communicate mood and effect – by voice and by instruments.	Experiment with voices: – high vocal sounds usually mean anxiety – low vocal sounds can be calming – short sounds give an element of surprise.
Recognising how music reflects the time and place in which it is written.	Make a collection of the children's and parents' favourite pieces of music. Listen and discuss. Were they written a long time ago? Can you hear anything to help you recognise their places of origin?

Appraising

Demonstrates an understanding of simple instructions – use of: f (loud), p (soft), raised hand.

Understands the changing character and mood of music (eg listens to a piece of music and responds to its changes through dance).

Nursery/Reception

Describes sounds heard in the classroom made by themselves and others.

Describes sounds heard in the environment.

Knows and understands that music has its own language (eg looks carefully at the signs used in song books and recognises why they are there: $f\ p <\ >$).

THE PLANETS
SUITE

by Gustav Holst

After Tom heard 'Mars, the God of War' from The Planet's Suite, he drew a pencil sketch of this Roman war ship. A small group of children then created music to accompany it .... leader on the drum, scraping sounds for rowers, wind sounds from those blowing instruments and a tune created on a wooden flute.

Describes sounds heard in recorded music, building up a musical vocabulary.

Describes and responds to music that is composed by self or others in the classroom.

Uses musical knowledge to support views on compositions and performances.

Continues to develop a musical vocabulary to express ideas.

Listens and responds to performances of live music in a wider field, such as assemblies, concerts.

Makes judgements about old/new pieces of music and responds through drama/art.

Compares music from contrasting musical traditions.

Year 6

A PRIMARY TEACHER'S HANDBOOK – *Music*

Appraising

SKILLS	SUGGESTED ACTIVITIES
✋ Describing the classroom sounds using simple terms.	✋ Listen to and describe sounds, using words like: louder, quiet, getting louder, silence, high, low, sliding, fast, tinkling, rattling.
✋ Describing sounds heard in the environment using simple terms.	✋ Make a collection of taped sounds from the local environment and invite the children to describe them.
✋ Demonstrating an understanding of simple instructions.	✋ Decide on hand signals for high and low. Agree with the children that they will respond by (a) singing and (b) playing a tuned instrument in response to the signal.
✋ Understanding the changing character and moods of music.	✋ Invite the children to respond in dance and movement to a variety of pieces (eg *Coppélia* by Clement Delibes (toy music), 'The Swan', *Carnival of the Animals* by Camille Saint-Saëns).
✋ Knowing and understanding that music has its own language and beginning to use this.	✋ Make flashcards with f (loud), p (soft), $<$ (getting louder), $>$ (getting softer). Invite response when these cards are shown at random. Create games using these. Try the same for high/low/long/short.
✋ Describing sounds heard in recorded music.	✋ Begin by listening to short pieces. Recognise the introduction, anything that is repeated, what the beat is, how the music ends, if the song is all vocal or sometimes instrumental.
✋ Describing and responding to own and others' compositions.	✋ During all composing activities, stop and start the children, and invite them to respond to another group's compositions.
✋ Listening and responding to live performances in a wider field – assemblies.	✋ Invite some children to act as newspaper reporters, writing down their views and opinions of school musical activities. Make a 'Musical Review' newspaper.
✋ Comparing music from contrasting musical traditions.	✋ Look at the musical traditions within the school – British, Divali, Christmas, Chanukkah. Discuss the similarities and differences. Remember sea shanties, spirituals, work songs, playground chants. Discuss the variety of instruments.
✋ Making judgements about old/new music, responding through drama/art.	✋ Listen to music from all ages and respond through drama and art.
✋ Continuing to develop a music vocabulary to express ideas.	✋ Recognise that music can be written down in many ways – traditional notation/graphic notation.
✋ Using musical knowledge to support views on compositions and performances.	✋ Encourage the children to have an opinion about music – classroom, visiting artists, recorded music, television music.

Providing experience

Pitch (high or low)

Many music activities will involve all the elements: pitch, duration and so on. Sometimes, however, it is useful to isolate one and to explore it more fully. The activities in this section of the handbook are suggestions for work on each element.

- Invite the children to listen to the sounds around them. Which are high, low, getting higher or lower? Ask pairs of children to re-create two of the sounds they have heard using their voices as well as body percussion and instruments. Encourage experiments with a variety of instruments. Listen and discuss.
- Make a collection of instruments. Ask the children to place them in groups of high, low, or both. Use these groups to portray:
  - climbing trees
  - diving into water
  - hopping in grass
  - jumping into puddles.
- Experiment with instruments that make sliding sounds – voices, recorders, xylophones, whistles. Create a game of 'Snakes and Ladders'. Draw a large square chart on which the children can add snakes and ladders. Choose two players to throw a dice. The rest of the class are divided into snakes (sliding sounds), ladders (tuned percussion) and empty squares (tambourines and drums). The players move around the board to the accompaniment of the instrumentalists.
- Ask the children to sing or play and follow the hand of a conductor as it curves up and down.
- Use the score below, 'Sing a score', with a conductor pointing to the curving line and the class responding.

- Discover a pentatonic scale (CDEGA). Place these notes on a tuned percussion instrument. Ask pairs of children to play 'Questions and Answers' (one child plays a short tune and the other answers it with a different tune) or 'Echoes' (one child makes up and plays a simple tune and his or her partner copies it).
- Invite small groups of children to experiment with musical leaps. They could describe:
  - a donkey braying
  - kangaroos hopping
  - frogs jumping.
- It is important that children learn a little of western notation. Make a chart of the notes on a scale, such as the one below, and encourage the children to learn them.

Sing a score

A PRIMARY TEACHER'S HANDBOOK – *Music*

Duration (long, short, beat, rhythm)

- Make a class list of the long and short sounds that are heard in the environment.
- Experiment with all instruments to find which will make long sounds and which will make short sounds.
- In a circle, pass round a long or short sound.
- Discover how to dampen the sound of an instrument by using a beater or a hand.
- Divide the class into four different machine sounds:
  - Bang
  - Yum chic Yum chic
  - Beedidee Beedidee
  - Wheeeeeeeeeeeepop.

  Each group should practise separately. Put two together, then three, then four. Stop and start at a given signal.
- Make an instrument that plays in free time, neither short nor long (eg a wind chime).
- With the whole class sitting in a circle, a leader begins to:
  - knee tap a steady beat, everyone follows
  - pass on a steady beat
  - change the beat and pass it on.
- Divide these instruments between the class: drum, tambour, woodblock, triangle. Agree that some children will play two beats, some three, some four and others five. Invite a conductor into the centre of the circle to point randomly at players to play their own rhythm.
- Write four phrases on the blackboard. They could be television programmes or football teams. The children should stand in a line, one behind the other. The person at the back chooses one of the phrases and taps the rhythm on the shoulder in front. This action is repeated until the rhythm reaches the front. Can the person at the front guess the phrase?
- Ask the children to make a list of well-known places in London. Tap out their rhythm together.
- Write out a clap-click-stamp chart such as that below. Ask the children to clap, click and stamp out the symbols together.

Get to know them (simple time)		
Quaver	♪	Half beat
Crotchet	♩	One beat
Dotted crotchet	♩.	One and a half beats
Minim	𝅗𝅥	Two beats
Dotted minim	𝅗𝅥.	Three beats
Semibreve	𝅝	Four beats

Clap (✱) Click (●) Stamp (■)				
Clap-click-stamp box				
start ● ● ✱ ✱	■ ■ ✱ ●	✱ ● ■ ■	■ ✱ ●	✱ ✱ ✱ ✱
● ● ● ●	■ ● ■ ●	(silence)	✱ ● ■ ✱	■ ● ✱ ✱ end

Tempo (fast and slow)

- ✋ Standing in a circle with the children, invite them to march to a steady beat with you. Now move faster or slower. Can they follow you?
- ✋ Make a collection of clocks for the children to listen to. Discuss the tempo of each clock's tick – is it fast or slow? Choose suitable instruments to copy the ticking clocks and create a piece called 'The Clock Shop'.
- ✋ Listen to *Carnival of the Animals* by Saint-Saëns to hear how a composer uses a variety of tempos to create the impression of animal movement – fish (quick), elephant (slow), swan (slow), tortoise (very slow).
- ✋ Tell the story of *The Hare and the Tortoise* with the children responding on instruments appropriate to each animal.

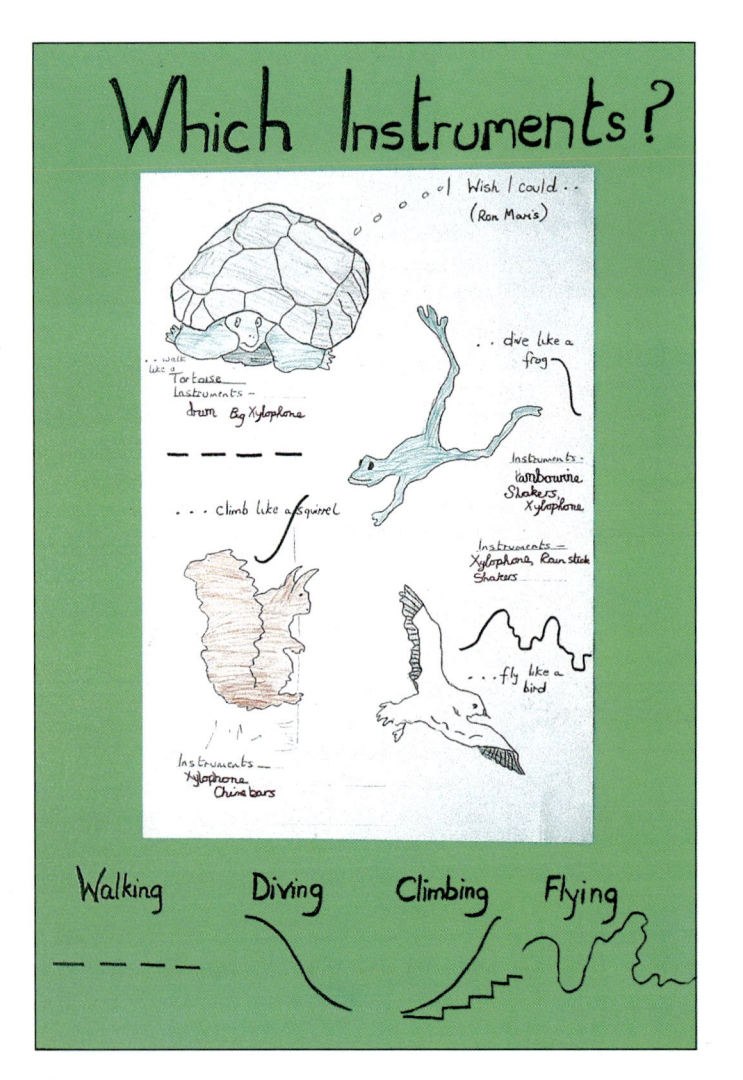

- ✋ Discuss different toy movements:
  - dancing doll
  - clockwork soldier
  - jack in the box
  - racing car
  - rockets.

  Ask the children to use different tempos to describe the toys musically. Create a toy rondo.
- ✋ Ask the children to keep in time with a metronome. Change the speed.
- ✋ Using a portable tape recorder let the children tape fast and slow sounds that they hear in the environment – footsteps, cars, clocks, horses.
- ✋ Ask pairs of children to make a musical sandwich (ABA, in which A would be a fast piece and B would be a slow piece). Listen to the contrasts. This is ternary form.
- ✋ Create a simple, slow ostinato with the children (a repeated tune, eg see-saw see-saw see-saw). It can be sung, said or played. Divide the group into two. Group one keeps the slow ostinato moving while the other group chants or plays the rhythm of the faster complete nursery rhyme, 'See-Saw Marjorie Dore'. Change over.
- ✋ Play two contrasting pieces of music to the children. They could be calm or stormy, fast or slow, played or sung. Invite the children to respond to the music's tempo through dance.

A PRIMARY TEACHER'S HANDBOOK – *Music*

Dynamics (soft, loud, soft to loud)

✋ Start with the sounds of words. Use the flashcards below (see the photocopiable flashcards on pages 54–55) and ask the children to find words that these symbols represent. For example, a word that explodes could be 'crash' and a word that hisses could be 'steam'.

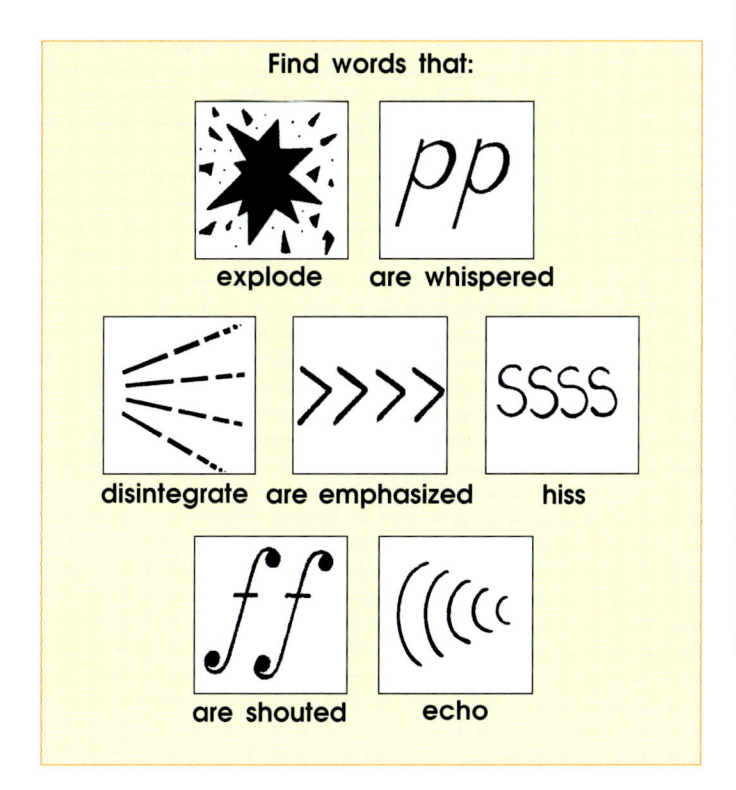

Find words that:
explode   are whispered
disintegrate   are emphasized   hiss
are shouted   echo

✋ Ask the children how they would say the words below – loudly, softly, getting louder.

✋ Give the children an opportunity to explore the best way to play instruments – softly or loudly.

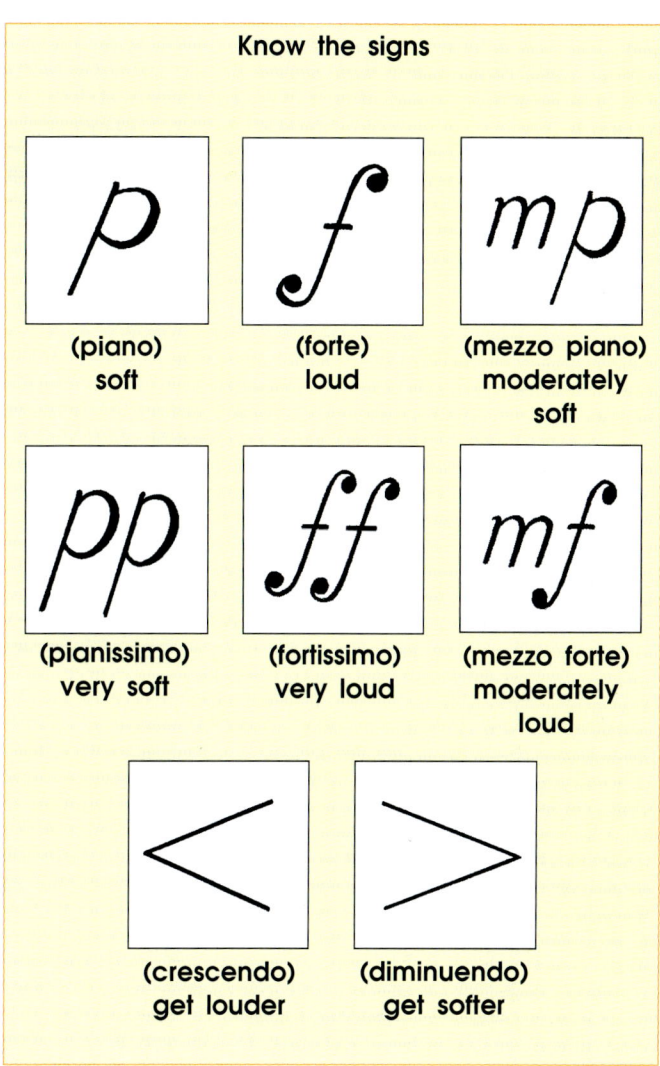

Know the signs

(piano) soft   (forte) loud   (mezzo piano) moderately soft

(pianissimo) very soft   (fortissimo) very loud   (mezzo forte) moderately loud

(crescendo) get louder   (diminuendo) get softer

Show them how different beaters (wire, wooden) will affect the sound on tuned percussion instruments. Different playing techniques will also change the sound – loose hold, firm hold, dragging, stroking, rolling, repeating and dampening.

✋ Agree on hand signals for soft, loud, very soft, very loud, getting louder, getting softer. Ask the children to use their voices or instruments to respond to signals given by the conductor.

✋ Make a number of flashcards as above. (See pages 56–57 for photocopiable flashcards.) Invite the children to respond with instruments as the conductor points to the cards.

✋ Some most effective music is written by contrasting loud and soft sounds. Ask the children to discover which instruments can get louder and which instruments can get softer. Invite the children to play the instruments and discuss their findings. Are there some instruments that never change? (These ideas can be used for creating music about trains, aeroplanes, whistling kettles.)

Timbre (sound quality)

- Ask each child to say their own name. Each voice will have a different sound. Ask the children to close their eyes. Can the children identify the voice of the speaking person when their shoulder is tapped?
- Choose a wide variety of instruments – tinkling, smooth, ringing, rattling, metal, wooden, skin. Listen to the different sounds each makes.
- From behind a screen or inside a box, play one instrument. Can the children identify the timbre?
- Discuss the differences in acoustic sound (natural sound) and electronic sound (electrical sound). Use the piano, electronic keyboard and guitar as examples. Compare old and new recordings to hear the differences in sound. The early pop music would not have had an electronic backing.
- The timbre of music from other cultures (Africa, Spain, India, China, England) will

depend on the different instruments used. Make a collection of recordings or borrow instruments for the children to identify these different sounds. Listen to short, taped pieces of music. Can the children identify the country from the timbre?
- Ask four children to each choose an instrument. They should be taken from different families – wood, metal, skin, shaken, banged. The whole

class sits with closed eyes and hears them played together. One stops – which is it?
- Each instrument of the orchestra has a different timbre. Listen to Britten's *Young Person's Guide to the Orchestra* to identify these sounds.
- Take three tuned instruments. Choose the same note on each to be played (for example, G on a chime bar, G on a xylophone, and G on a metallophone). Ask one child to play them in the same order over and over again while the rest of the class listens. The instruments could be hidden. Number the instruments one, two, three. Ask the player to miss one out. Which is it? Now ask them to play one only. Can the children identify which instrument is being played?
- Make short recordings of voices singing (a soprano, a contralto, a tenor, a bass, a country and western and a folk singer). The children should listen to the different sounds of their voices and link the sound with the type of voice.

Texture (several sounds together)

- Choose four different sounding instruments and four players. Let the children play a march rhythm together. Now ask the group to move out of sight of the other class members. One player must stop playing, and the children should detect which instrument sound is missing.

- Each child should have one untuned instrument. The children must then group themselves in wood/metal/skin groups. Give each group a word pattern to play:
  – I like toast
  – Sausages for me
  – My dad likes porridge.
  Gradually build up each – sound on sound/phrase on phrase.

- Well-known songs and rounds can be made more interesting by adding a simple accompaniment. For *Three Blind Mice*, ask the children to start on a low E and work out the tune. Accompany this with a repeated tune of low C followed by high C or both Cs played together. The theme tune to *Eastenders* begins on a C and can be accompanied by playing a repeated pattern of GC.

- Weave vocal sounds together by singing descants or easy second tunes to hymns and well-known songs.

- Ask small groups of children to create a football chant, a playground chant or a school games chant. Perform by asking one voice to begin and gradually change the texture as more join in.

- Different voices can be brought together in the firework music below. The class should be divided into small groups of five people. This will enable one child in each group to conduct the four voices.

- Many songs and rounds can be accompanied by simple chords (more than one note). Often chords have three notes. Ask pairs of children to choose a chord (CEG, GBD or ACE). One player plays a steady rhythm on three chime bars, while the other improvises on the same three notes on any tuned percussion instrument. They should then change over.

- Divide the class into shakers, bangers, rattlers, blowers, each with an instrument. The conductor points to each group to perform a piece called 'A Stormy Day At Sea'.

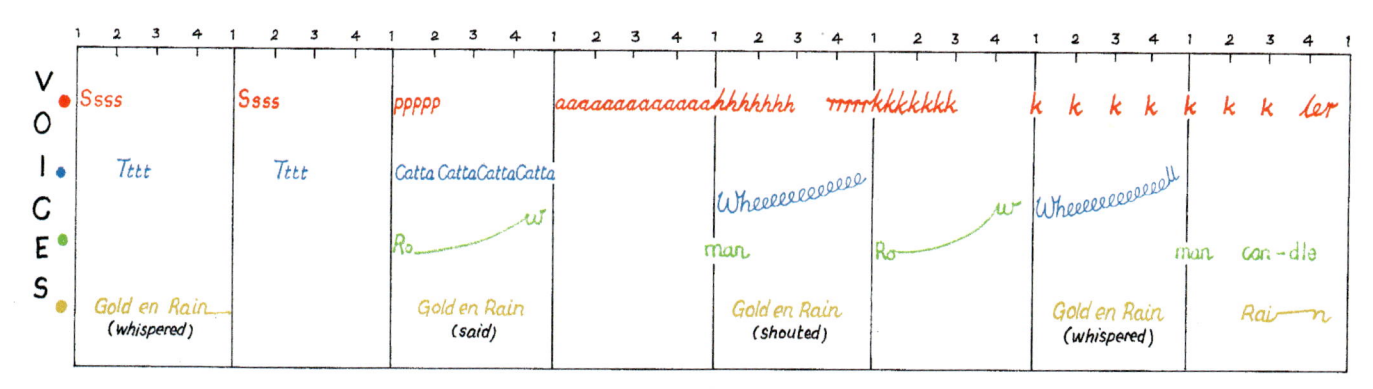

Structure (how music is put together)

- Discuss with the children how music has a beginning, a middle and an end, just like a story or a poem. Look at, and listen to, short pieces of music or songs to identify this.

- Pairs of children could create a piece of music where one tune is repeated. Player one could play an ostinato on any instrument, while player two improvises above that sound.

- Take any well-known story (eg *The End of the Road* by Hilaire Belloc) and retell it musically in a structured interpretation. For example:
  - choose certain instruments for special characters
  - record environmental sounds as sound effects
  - discuss the movement of the characters (running/ hopping/jumping/flying).

  Invite the children to respond to the story with their instruments.

- With the whole class in a circle, the leader claps a rhythm pattern (♫ ♩ ♩ ♩). Everyone copies. The leader changes the pattern but the class stays unchanged until the leader says 'fudge'. Everyone should now be together again. The leader then changes again making the new rhythm as difficult as the class can manage.

- Children's own poetry and that of well-known poets lends itself to a structured musical accompaniment. For example, 'The Owl', by Alfred Tennyson, and 'Sea Shell' by Enid Madoc-Jones (*Word Games*). Descriptive musical sounds played as sensitively as the poem is read can be most effective, Poems with a chorus, such as 'The Lamb', by William Blake and 'It's Winter, It's Winter' by Kit Wright (*More Word Games*), lend themselves to tune composing on the tuned percussion instruments (see page 61 for some photocopiable poetry).

- When singing well-known songs, encourage the singers to sing a whole phrase in one breath. This will be marked: ⌒ .

- A clock rondo. Divide the class into small groups, each one working out a piece of music to describe a specific clock. Put them together in a rondo, as shown below.

A	B	A	C	A	D	A
Big Ben	Wrist watch	Big Ben	Cuckoo clock	Big Ben	Alarm clock	Big Ben

A PRIMARY TEACHER'S HANDBOOK – *Music*

Notation (writing down music)

- ☝ Choose a variety of instruments. Explore with the children the different ways of playing them.
- ☝ Place a large sheet of paper in the centre of the class circle. Play one sound on any instrument and investigate whether anyone can write a symbol to represent the sound. Try more.
- ☝ Pairs of children should choose:
  - a vocal sound
  - a body sound
  - an untuned sound
  - a tuned sound.

  Child one plays or sings a sound and child two writes an appropriate symbol on a flashcard. The cards should be exchanged with another group for them to play.

- ☝ Make some flashcards (see below for examples) showing a variety of symbols. Decide with the children how they could be played. In small groups let the children play the graphic notation.

- ☝ Discuss with the children the need to write down music to:
  - keep it for another day
  - pass on to other people.
- ☝ Both traditional and graphic notation are used in the western world.

Rests are very important in music. This is how some of them look.

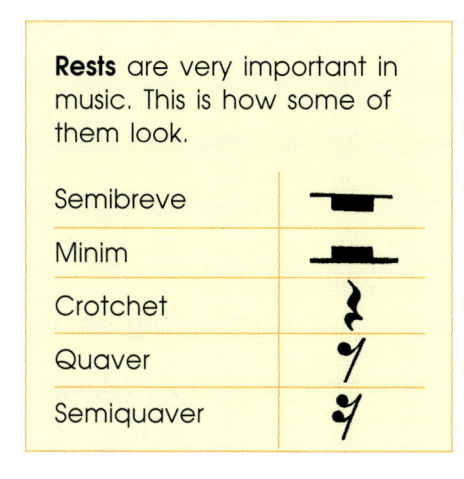

Semibreve	
Minim	
Crotchet	
Quaver	
Semiquaver	

Flashcard examples

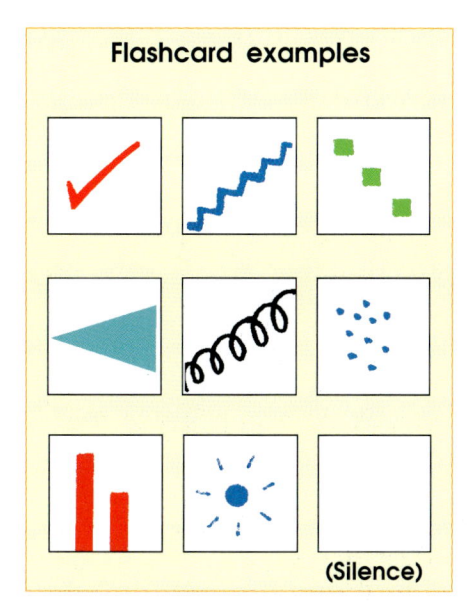

(Silence)

Traditional and graphic notation

C D E F G A B C

Guitar chords are written like this:

E A D G B E

Sing or play this score

START END

A PRIMARY TEACHER'S HANDBOOK – *Music*

Classroom practice

Planning

Teachers preparing to take a music lesson, need to create a good atmosphere in which the children feel able to create their music.

Agree on

What to agree on?
- When to listen.
- When to begin.
- When to stop.
- How long to experiment.
- Various signals.

Plan

What is the theme?
- Sounds around us.

Where will it move?
- **From** – exploration of sound in our environment.
- **To** – short pieces created by groups (eg 'The Haunted House').

Warm up activities – why?
- To get to know the group.
- To create group unity.
- To remind the children of previous activities.

Main activities – why?
- To explore sounds with others.
- To organise those sounds.
- To use the imagination.

How many sessions?
- As many as needed – maybe two each week for a term.

Who to perform to?
- Each other/other classes.

How to record it?
- In graphic notation/on a tape recorder/in traditional notation.

Lesson plan

Preparation
- Ideas/furniture/space/instruments.
- What else?

Starter activities
- How many?

Main activities
- How long?
- How many groups?

Play back
- To the teacher/to another group/to whole class.

Discussion
- What did you think? How can it be improved?

Final performance
- Try again and play back.

Move on

When to move on?
- As soon as you sense the children are ready.
- Integrate the work that you have done into a new theme or into a completely different area (eg another musical element).

Use of space

For group work

Pairs
- Can work in any space.

Small group
- Needs a designated area.

Whole group
- Needs space for a circle.

Beaters

Where?
- On a wall frame.
- In a large tin.
- Separated in boxes (felt heads, wooden heads, plastic) and colour coded.

When to distribute?
- Give them out after your instructions for the lesson.

The music area

How to organise?
- Begin each session with everyone sitting in a circle for the following reasons:
  - maintenance of eye contact
  - access to a small number of instruments in centre of circle
  - ease of communication.
- Designate areas for small group work.
- Make many instruments available from easily accessible places.

The classroom

How to organise?
- Move the furniture around to make a large enough space for all to sit in a circle.
- Make sure every child has eye contact with the leader.
- Place instruments in convenient areas for collection.
- Decide where small groups will work.

Instruments

Where?
- On a trolley near the teacher for easy distribution.
- Around the room (not all in one place).
- On a music table (selected groups, eg scraping sounds, wood, metal – change regularly).
- In the centre of the circle.
- In a cupboard, clearly marked.

Plan a lesson: Dynamics (soft and loud)

Preparation

- Prepare a large enough space for everyone to sit in a circle.
- Gather together a large number of instruments.
- Have large sheets of paper and thick pens to hand.
- Make flashcards – p and f.

Introduction

- In a circle the leader taps knees in steady beat. The children join in (soft/loud).
- Change to:
  - clicking fingers (p–f)
  - clapping hands (f–p)
  - tapping feet (p–f–p).
- Sing 'clap, click, stamp'.
- Ask for silence.
- What can be heard?

Make a chart

p (soft)	f (loud)
Whisper	Door banging

- Explain p and f.
- Use flashcards – p and f. Ask the children to respond vocally on seeing a card and then by using body percussion.

Small groups/pairs

- Invite pairs of children to think of phrases for p and f such as:
  - 'Baby's sleeping'
  - 'Come back Tom'.
- Report back to the whole class.

Whole group again

- Give out tuned and untuned instruments.
- On agreed signals play p and f.
- Note the different techniques for each.

Main activity

- Divide into smaller groups (4–6). Aim to use p and f in a musical piece.
- Choose a title from: 'Bedtime'/'The Mouse'/'Storms'/'Saturday Shopping'/'Wind Chimes'/'Balloon Burst'. Suggest a beginning/middle/end pattern. Will it be p–f–p pattern or f–p–f.
- Give a time limit to create short pieces.
- Play to one another.
- Discuss and tape.

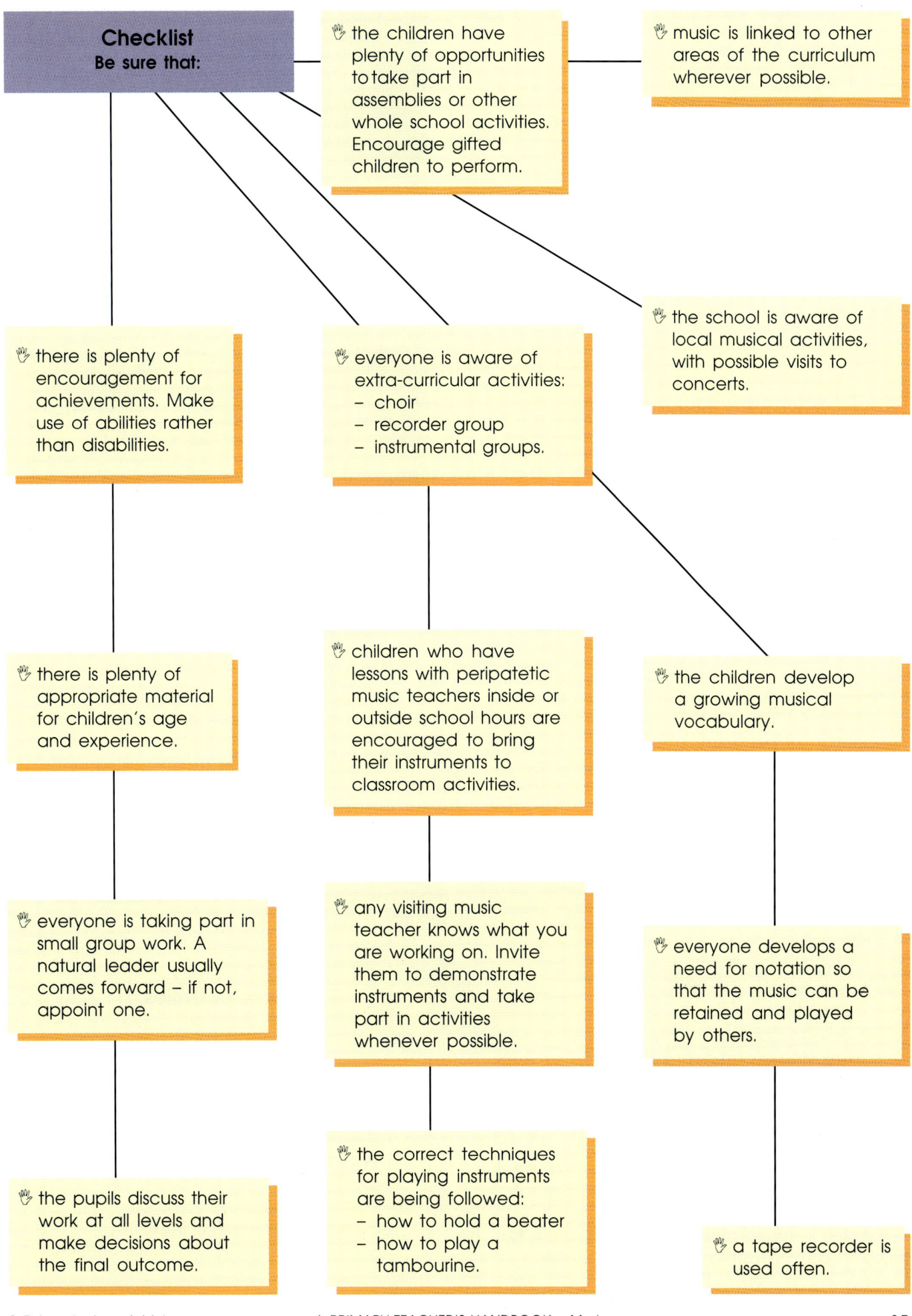

Checklist
Be sure that:

🖐 the children have plenty of opportunities to take part in assemblies or other whole school activities. Encourage gifted children to perform.

🖐 music is linked to other areas of the curriculum wherever possible.

🖐 the school is aware of local musical activities, with possible visits to concerts.

🖐 there is plenty of encouragement for achievements. Make use of abilities rather than disabilities.

🖐 everyone is aware of extra-curricular activities:
– choir
– recorder group
– instrumental groups.

🖐 there is plenty of appropriate material for children's age and experience.

🖐 children who have lessons with peripatetic music teachers inside or outside school hours are encouraged to bring their instruments to classroom activities.

🖐 the children develop a growing musical vocabulary.

🖐 everyone is taking part in small group work. A natural leader usually comes forward – if not, appoint one.

🖐 any visiting music teacher knows what you are working on. Invite them to demonstrate instruments and take part in activities whenever possible.

🖐 everyone develops a need for notation so that the music can be retained and played by others.

🖐 the pupils discuss their work at all levels and make decisions about the final outcome.

🖐 the correct techniques for playing instruments are being followed:
– how to hold a beater
– how to play a tambourine.

🖐 a tape recorder is used often.

Special needs

Gifted children

The child with exceptional music skills needs to be identified as soon as possible. Often this is brought to the school's attention by parents who may seek advice about specialist music.

Non-musical parents, however, sometimes find it hard to recognise and accept the abilities of a gifted child and so the classroom teacher plays an important role.

Most educational authorities have peripatetic instrumental teachers who are based centrally. They would be willing to meet the child, assess their ability, direct them towards available opportunities and help them find an instrument (often available to be hired).

It is important for the school to support this teaching by creating opportunities for these pupils to perform in the classroom, during assemblies or in school concerts. Playing in isolation is of little benefit to the pupil. The introduction of peripatetic music teachers to the school environment can be an added bonus to the classroom teacher if they are encouraged to become part of the school's music curriculum.

By concentrating on children's abilities rather than their disabilities they can be brought 'one step nearer to the achievements of able-bodied youngsters'.

Creative and re-creative music-making in the classroom helps all children to express their emotions, aids language development and general coordination.

Singing can help those who have speech difficulties, in particular those who stutter, and repetitive songs foster a much needed sense of security.

Look out for

Pupils who are:
- very enthusiastic about music
- able to sing well, in tune, and remember the music
- able to compose easily
- enjoying a particular instrument.

Try these activities

- Cover the holes on a recorder so that only the ones needed can be played.
- Have three children playing one chime bar, each of the same note to give added confidence.
- Encourage children to conduct. It can easily be done from a wheelchair.
- Place uncertain singers by more confident ones to boost their confidence.

Other special educational needs

It has long since been proved that children with special educational needs respond well to music and music-making. They can achieve a great deal of success.

'Success in music making often sparks off the desire to attempt other activities.' (*They Can Make Music* by Bailey (1973))

Information technology

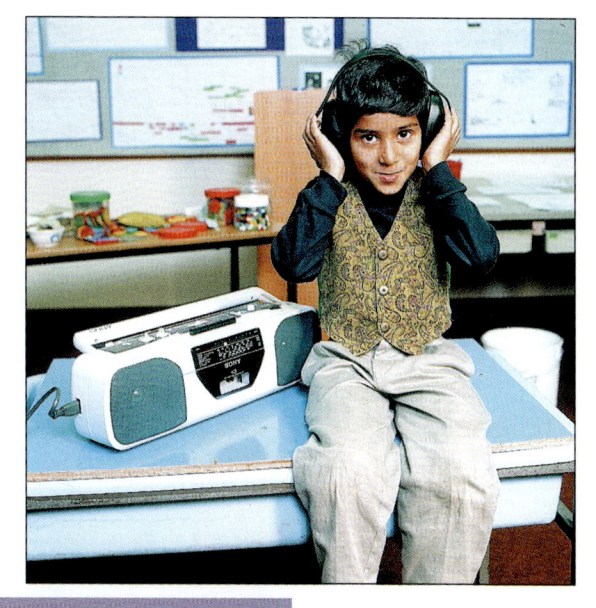

Programme of Study

Pupils should be given the opportunity to make appropriate use of IT to record sound.

Key Stage 1

- Use a cassette recorder to tape sounds from the environment to use in compositions.
- Use a microphone.
- Respond to fast/slow sounds on tape.
- Tape own work and that of other people.
- Look at and listen to children's musical toys. How do they work?
- Tape two short tunes (A and B) and place them in the beginning, middle or end structure (ABA).
- Use taped sounds.
- Create a story to be spoken with taped background sounds.

Key Stage 2

- On a reel-to-reel tape recorder, experiment with the speed control to create effects.
- Experiment with electronic keyboards to create sliding sounds, leaping sounds, harsh sounds, mellow sounds.
- Experiment with karaoke.
- Use electronic keyboards to experiment with rhythms/beats:
  – play a rhythm (tap a tune/sing a tune/play a tune)
  – keep in time with the beat – tap your feet
  – find the first beat.
- Respond through dance, movement or art to a piece of recorded music.
- Use a computer program to create simple compositions.
- Create a musical rondo (ABACADA) using several groups' compositions and a tape recorder.
- Discover chords on a keyboard: CEG, GBD, FAC.
- Discuss differences between acoustic and electronic instruments.

Assessment

There are no nationally prescribed tests in music for Key Stages 1 and 2 but the Attainment Targets set out in the National Curriculum for music document are intended to describe the types and ranges of performance that the majority of pupils should characteristically demonstrate by the end of each Key Stage. The descriptions are designed to help teachers judge the extent to which their pupils' attainment relates to their expectations.

With so many non-specialists teaching music and with so many specialists being asked to act as consultants for a great many music lessons, assessment of music is often avoided. Assessment of music is both difficult and time consuming – difficult because in a well-planned music session all the listening, composing, performing and appraising skills are in action at the same time and cannot be assessed independently.

It is important, however, that some form of assessment takes place because teachers should be aware of how well the child is developing, in comparison with others of his or her age. This can be discussed with parents. It is also important in that it gives a guide to how successful the scheme of work has been.

On a day-to-day basis, the teacher will assess the pupil's understanding by observation and discussion – observation of how the child approaches a

task and discussion with the child about the outcome.

In the short term, activities and achievements could be recorded by a teacher or helper on a simple record sheet, or filing card. This would show the activity with comments, thus keeping an interesting, up-to-date account of the child's work.

A longer view (half-yearly or yearly) could be recorded by looking at more specific areas of the composing, performing, listening and appraising skills (as shown on the photocopiable page opposite).

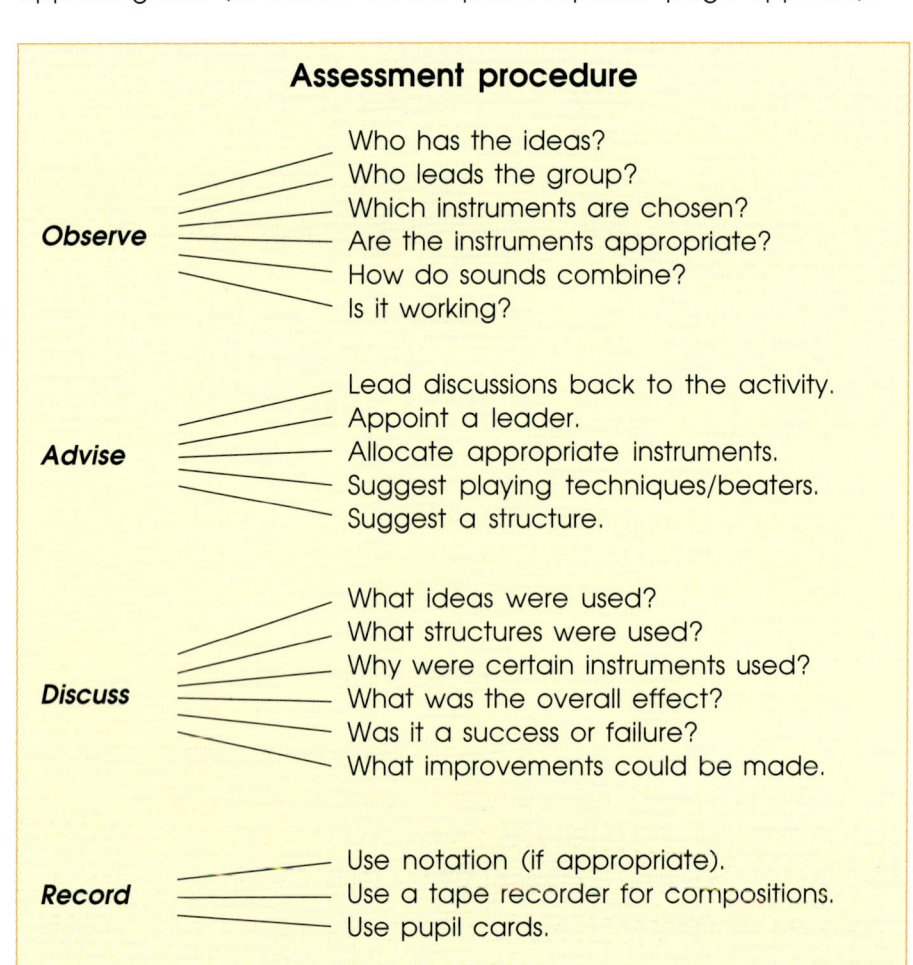

Assessment procedure

Observe
- Who has the ideas?
- Who leads the group?
- Which instruments are chosen?
- Are the instruments appropriate?
- How do sounds combine?
- Is it working?

Advise
- Lead discussions back to the activity.
- Appoint a leader.
- Allocate appropriate instruments.
- Suggest playing techniques/beaters.
- Suggest a structure.

Discuss
- What ideas were used?
- What structures were used?
- Why were certain instruments used?
- What was the overall effect?
- Was it a success or failure?
- What improvements could be made.

Record
- Use notation (if appropriate).
- Use a tape recorder for compositions.
- Use pupil cards.

A PRIMARY TEACHER'S HANDBOOK – *Music*

Assessment chart

Record of achievement	N A M E S													
Good ✳	Average ✔	Has difficulty ✗												
Year group														
Key Stage														
COMPOSING														
Is able to compose														
Selects/explores sounds														
Uses voice/instruments														
Creates musical patterns														
Uses notation – graphic/traditional														
Improvises														
Uses structures														
PERFORMING														
Performs with confidence														
Is aware of others														
Performs on instruments														
Performs vocally														
Performs from memory														
Performs from notation														
LISTENING														
Listens to environmental sounds														
Listens to others														
Listens to recorded music														
Responds through art														
Responds through dance/drama														
APPRAISING														
Discusses with others														
Uses a musical vocabulary														
Responds to live performances														
Has a musical opinion														
USE OF INFORMATION TECHNOLOGY														
ENTHUSIASM														
SPECIAL TALENTS														
CLUBS/CHOIR														

Listening links

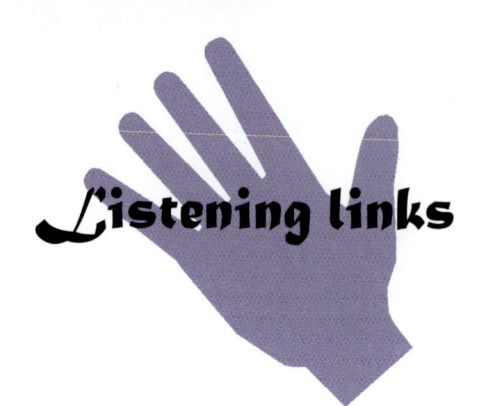

Pitch

🖐 Listen for the jumping music of the broom in *The Sorcerer's Apprentice* by Dukas.

🖐 The kangaroos hopping in *Carnival of the Animals* by Saint-Saëns.

🖐 The flow of the music up and down in 'Morning' from Grieg's *Peer Gynt*.

🖐 The sliding sounds in 'Prelude' from Kodály's *Háry János* suite.

Duration

🖐 Listen for the regular beats in *The Syncopated Clock* by Leroy Anderson and 'The Clock' symphony by Haydn. Also 'Viennese Clock' from *Háry Janos* suite by Kodály.

Timbre

🖐 Listen to the sound of voices – Pavarotti, Carreras, Cliff Richard, Madonna – and hear the differences.

🖐 *Young Person's Guide to the Orchestra* by Britten will show you all the sounds of orchestral instruments.

Dynamics

🖐 Ravel's *Boléro* gradually gets louder.

🖐 Haydn's 'Surprise' symphony (2nd Mov.) is quiet (p) and then loud (f).

🖐 Holst's 'Mars' from *The Planets* suite gradually gets louder.

🖐 In Grieg's 'Hall of the Mountain King' from *Peer Gynt* hear the music getting louder.

Tempo

🖐 Listen to the slow music in 'The Tortoise' and the fast music of the quick animals in Saint-Saëns, *Carnival of the Animals*.

🖐 Hear the lively music of 'Jupiter', the bringer of jollity, from Holst's *The Planets*.

Texture

🖐 Hear the special music for each character of *Peter and the Wolf* by Prokofiev
– Peter – string quartet
– cat – clarinet
– wolf – bassoon.

Structure

🖐 Hear the ternary form (ABA) loud/soft/loud in *The Sabre Dance* by Katchaturian.

A PRIMARY TEACHER'S HANDBOOK – *Music*

The weather

- Ludwig Van Beethoven – 'Storm', Symphony No. 6
- Benjamin Britten – 'Four Sea Interludes', *Peter Grimes*
- Benjamin Britten – *Noyes Fludde*
- Frederick Delius – *On Hearing the First Cuckoo in Spring*
- Edward Grieg – 'Morning', *Peer Gynt*
- Felix Mendelssohn – *Fingal's Cave*
- Modeste Mussorgsky – *Night on the Bare Mountain*
- Antonio Vivaldi – *The Four Seasons*

Sounds

- Benjamin Britten – *Young Person's Guide to the Orchestra*
- Gustav Holst – *The Planets* suite (slow sustained sounds followed by short fast sounds)
- Penderecki – *Hiroshima* (unusual sounds)
- Camille Saint-Saëns – *Carnival of the Animals* (pianists)
- Karlheinz Stockhausen – *Kontakte* (electronic sounds)
- Peter Ilich Tchaikovsky – *1812 Overture* (cannon sounds at the end)

Machines

- Leroy Anderson – *The Typewriter*
- Joseph Haydn – 'The Clock'
- Arthur Honegger – *Pacific 231*
- Heitor Villa-Lobos – *The Little Train*
- Claus Wunderlich – *Dance of the Automatons*

Animals

- Benjamin Britten – *Noye's Fludde*
- Aaron Copland – *Rodeo*
- Gerry Goldsmith – *Planet of the Apes*
- J Horvitz – *Captain Noah and his Floating Zoo*
- Modeste Mussorgsky – *Pictures at an Exhibition*
- Sergey Prokofiev – *Peter and the Wolf*
- Camille Saint-Saëns – *Carnival of the Animals*
- Igor Stravinsky – *The Firebird*

Music from other cultures

Country	Title	Composer
China	*Yellow River Concerto*	Popular Chinese Orchestra
England	*Pomp and Circumstance*	Edward Elgar
Finland	*Finlandia*	Jean Sibelius
Greece	*Zorba's Dance*	Theodorakis
India	*Within You, Without You* (Indian style)	The Beatles
	Music from India	Ravi Shankar
Israel	*Fiddler on the Roof*	Sheldon Harnick/Jerry Bock
	Jeremiah symphony	Leonard Bernstein
Russia	Polovtsian Dances	Alexander Borodin
	Gopak	Modeste Mussorgsky
Scotland	*The Bluebell Polka*	Jimmy Shand
South Africa	*Ipi N Tombi*	Egnor/Lakier
Spain	*España*	Emmanuel Chabrier
West Indies	*Get up, Stand up*	Bob Marley

Themes and musical links

Here are two different ways of approaching project work through music.

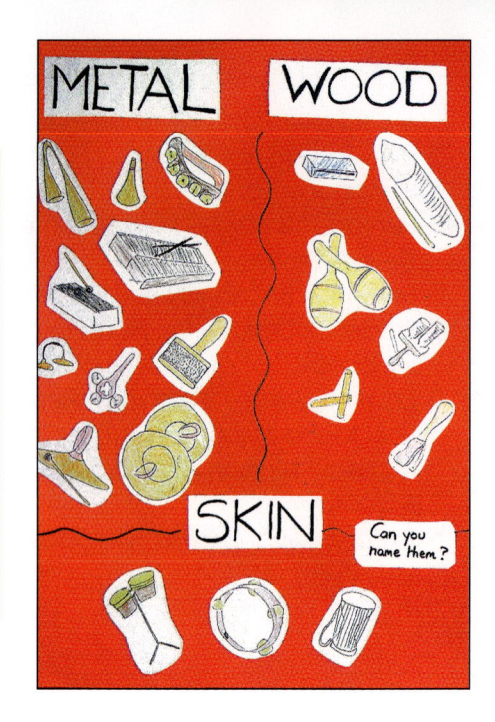

Starter activities

- Listen to sounds in the environment – high/low/long/short. Make lists, experiment with instruments and use flashcards p and f.
- Create vocal sounds.
- Play body percussion games: 'Echo', 'Fudge', 'Questions and Answers', 'Names'.
- Experience vibrations.

Creative activities

- Explore the timbre of the instruments:
  - metal/wood/skin
  - wind/string/brass
  - electronic sounds
  - instruments from other lands.
- Create music called 'The Haunted House':
  - experiment with water in glasses
  - invent instruments, eg wind chimes
  - explore the sounds of paper.

Sounds

Re-creative activities

- Accompany songs with simple accompaniments.
- Many of the song books recommended at the end of this guide will give a wide range of accompaniments, ranging from the very easy to the more difficult.

Starter activities

- Use long and short sounds to create machine sounds. Measure vibrations of instruments. Use a stop-watch. Experiment with a metronome. Pass a vocal machine sound around a circle.

Creative activities

- Invent musical machine pieces for the home/country/school/city. Create a bizarre factory where some machine music goes wrong. Create a time rondo/machine rondo/fairground rondo.
- Invent a toy and describe it musically.

Machines

Re-creative activities

- Accompany songs with simple accompaniments.
- Look at the suggested song bank on page 44–45 to find accompaniments (both simple and more difficult).

People around us

- Sing a name game. Create a name score or sing the register. Improvise on the song 'When I grow up I'd like to be ...'

Favourite poems

- Decide which poems could be sung. Which ones have a chorus? Could background music be appropriate?
- Write a poem and use a pentatonic scale to write a tune.

Our school

- Take a well-known tune and write new words that fit, eg 'Our School Song'.

Machines we use

- Create music for machines in the office, the home and the street. Re-create machine adverts using voices and body percussion. Add instrumental accompaniments to vocal machine sounds.

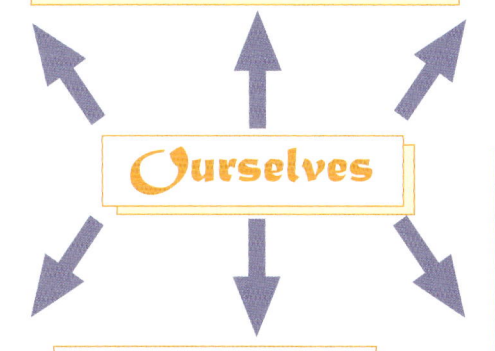

Ourselves

Our traditions

- Find out about any unusual traditions from other cultures.
- Discover music for our own traditions – Christmas/Easter/Bonfire Night.

Sounds around us

- Listen and keep a record of sounds in our own environment. Re-create these using the elements.

Food

- Create word patterns about food likes and dislikes – fish and chips/bread and butter.
- Put the word patterns together to make a musical menu.

Hot and cold

- Which instruments sound cold (metal or wood)? Hot? Divide the instruments into two groups – hot and cold – and create a tune of contrasts.

The sun and the wind

- Draw a graphic score creating a piece of 'Wind and Waves on the Sea' music.
- Write some poems and accompany them with instruments.

Energy

Devices

- Look inside a piano and see how it works. Notice the hammers, the dampers and the pedal action.

Power sources

- Compare and contrast electronic sounds with acoustic (natural) sounds.
- Create simple instruments using rubber bands, wood, cartons, bells and so on.

Toys

- Discuss the mechanical toys in a toyshop. How did they work in the past? How do they work today? Create music to describe some toys – dancing dolls, toy soldiers, racing cars, rockets. Let one group move/dance to the music created by another group.

Song banks

These two pages feature songbooks that contain songs for use in a range of different topic areas.

Energy

Flying a Round
Kites Flying High
Row the Boat
Blow the Wind Southerly
Little Wind
Beware the Force of Gravity
Things that Go Bump
Sound Waves
Zum Galli
Gently into Music
Jig Jog
Granny's Yard
Keep the Food Mills Turning
Jolly Herring
Football Crazy
Sing a Story
Charlie and the Chocolate Factory
Ta-ra-ra Boom-de-ay
The Runaway Train
My Grandfather's Clock

Festivals

Carol, Gaily Carol
A wide selection of carols
Gently into Music
Harvest
Halloween
Fireworks
A Musical Calendar of Festivals
Pancake Tuesday
Mothering Sunday
May Garlands
Havah Nagilah
America (Independence Day)
Vreneli (Swiss National Day)
God Speed the Plough (Harvest)
Tzena (Jewish National Day)

Animals

Apusskidu
The Wombling Song
The Animals Went in Two by Two
The Bold Hippopotamus
Five Little Frogs
The Elephant
Game Songs
When a Dinosaur Feels Hungry
Walking Through the Jungle
Monster Stomp
Gently into Music
A Green Frog
Jig Jog
Kokoleoko
200 Million Years
Mrs Macaroni
I Went for a Walk One Day
Puff the Magic Dragon
Tyrannosaurus Rex
Phantasmagoria
Thunderbird
Unicorn
Griffin
Sing a Song Book 2
Nelly the Elephant

Colour

Allsorts
Sing a Rainbow
Apusskidu
Yellow Submarine
Little Brown Jug
Lily the Pink
Count me in
10 Green Bottles
Flying a Round
Brown Yellow Kiskidee
Game Songs
Colour Song
Granny's Yard
Black, White, Yellow and Green
I Went for a Walk
Hullabaloo-balay!
Cherry Pink and Apple Blossom White
Jolly Herring
The Yellow Rose of Texas
Kokoleoko
Red Flowers
Mrs Macaroni
Mary Wore a Red Dress
Traffic Lights

Machines

Allsorts
Tick Tock
Wheels on the Bus
Apusskidu
Yellow Submarine
Wheels Keep Turning
Morning Town Ride
Flying a Round
Ticking Clocks
To Stop the Train
Granny's Yard
Take you Riding
Hullabaloo-balay!
Garage Round
Runaway Train
I have a Song to Sing
Telephone Song
Jolly Herring
Casey Jones
Kokoleoko
I've Got an Engine
Mrs Macaroni
This Train is Bound for London
Phantasmagoria
The Grand Robot Sale

Sounds

Apusskidu
Whistle a Happy Tune
Every Colour Under the Sun
Use Your Eyes
If I Had a Hammer
Flying a Round
Music Is Fun
Clap, Stamp, Click
Calypso
Junkanoo
Game Songs
Sam Creep Up
His Name Is Pete
Sounds We Hear
Harlequin
Can You Hear?
Sing a Song Book 1
Clap Your Hands
Sing a Song Book 2
Clapping Hands

Ourselves

Apusskidu
If You're Happy
I'd Like to Teach the World to Sing
Boomps-a-daisy
Oh What a Beautiful Morning
Maybe It's Because I'm a Londoner
KKKKaty
Early Learning Centre
Heads and Shoulders
Gently into Music
Going on a Trip
My Hands Upon My Head
Two Soldiers
Who Has the Penny?
Okki-tokki-unga
Every Body Do This
Sing a Story
Open the Cover
Ta-ra-ra Boom-de-ay
When I'm 64
I'm Forever Blowing Bubbles

The weather

Allsorts
I Hear Thunder
Jack Frost
March Winds
Apusskidu
Sing a Rainbow
Every Colour Under the Sun
Morning Sun
Faber Music
Walking in the Air (The Snowman)
Flying a Round
Little Wind
Game Songs
Weather Songs
Harlequin
Snowflakes
Wonderful Weather
Umbrella Man
Fog
Jolly Herring
The Lightning Tree
Juke Box
Raining in My Heart
Catch a Falling Star
I Can See Clearly Now
Mrs Macaroni
Can You Tell Me?
Strawberry Fair
Blow the Wind

Tuned percussion

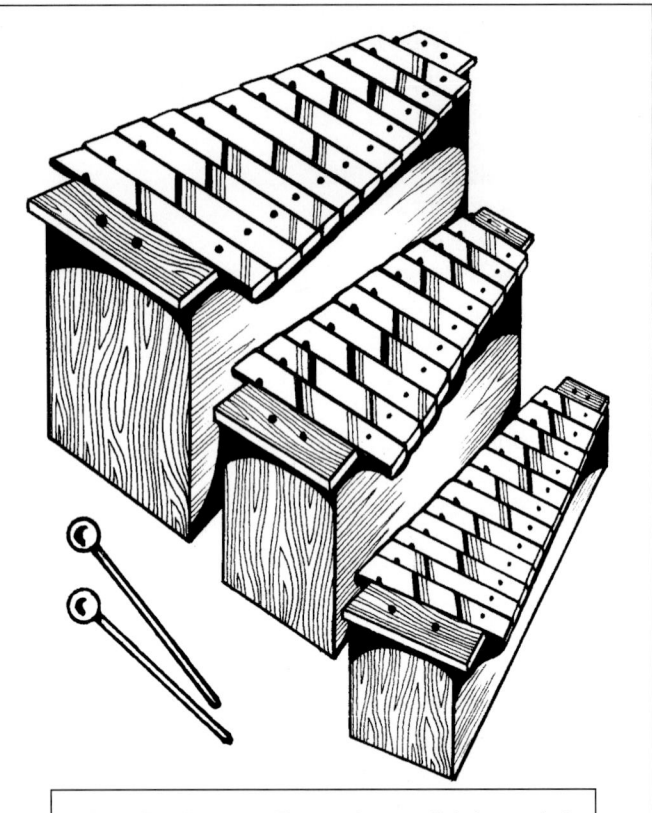

Metallophones. These have thick metal bars and a very resonant sound.

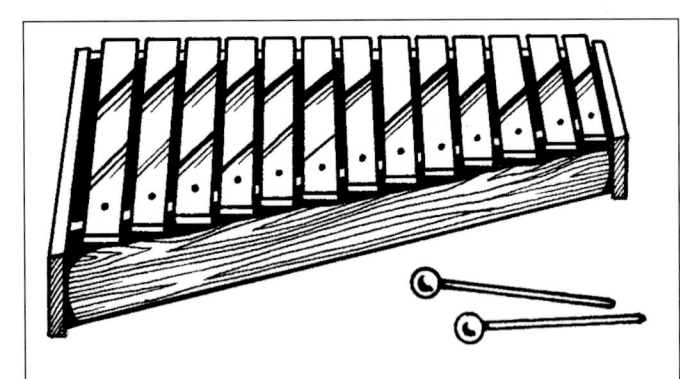

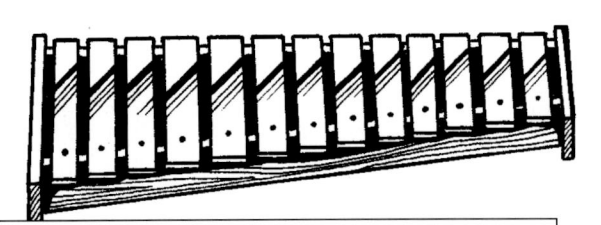

Glockenspiels. These are smaller than the xylophones and have thin metal bars which produce a bell-like sound.

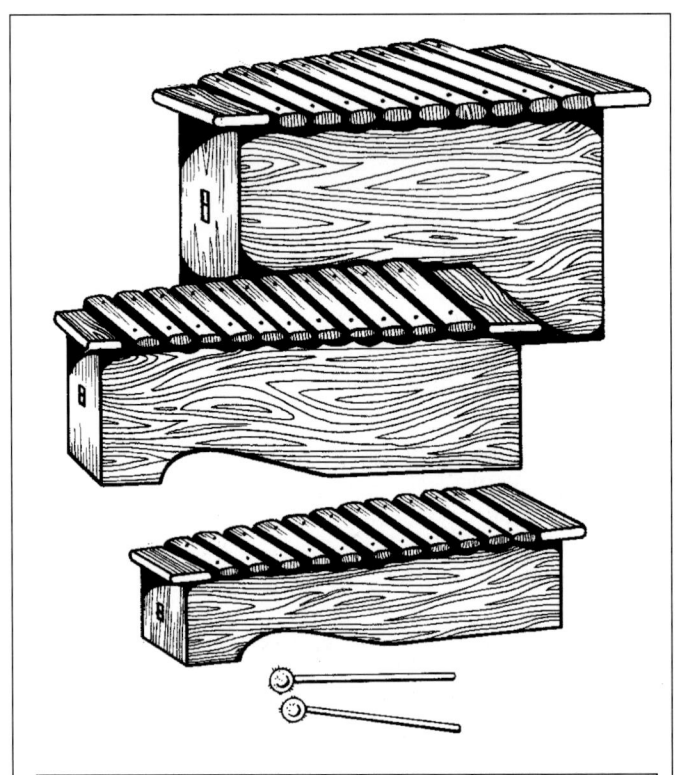

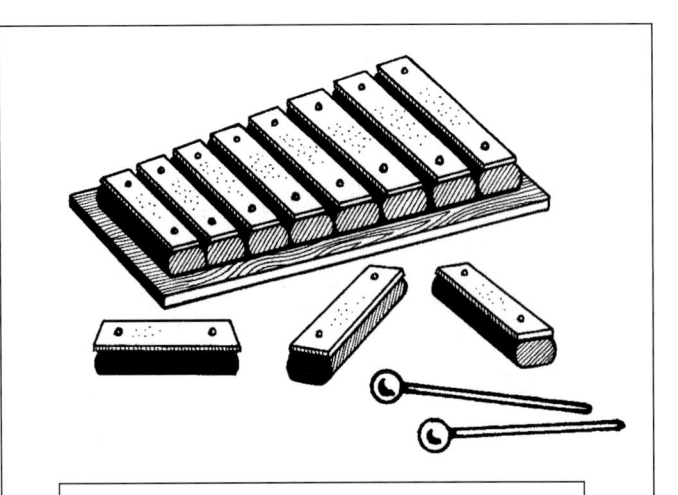

Chime bars. These usually have metal bars. They can be used as a set or divided up and used on their own.

Xylophones. These have wooden or glass fibre bars. The smallest instrument has the highest sound. The largest instrument has the lowest sound. Padded or wooden beaters can be used to create different effects.

A PRIMARY TEACHER'S HANDBOOK – *Music*

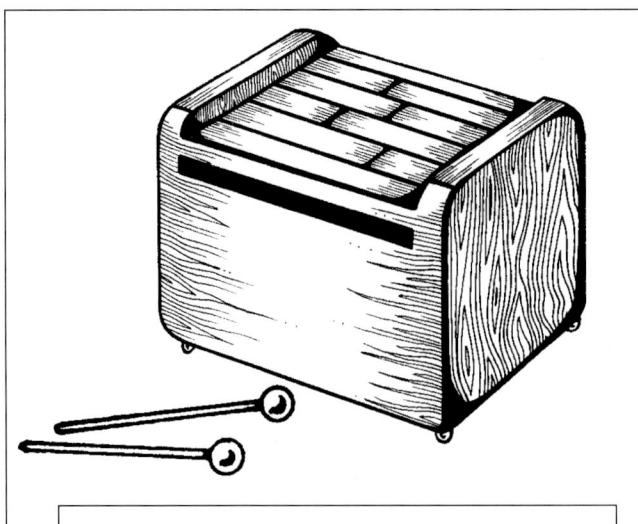

Gato drum. This wooden drum can play a variety of different pitches.

Handbells. Each bell is tuned to a different note. Players usually hold one in each hand and play with a small group of people.

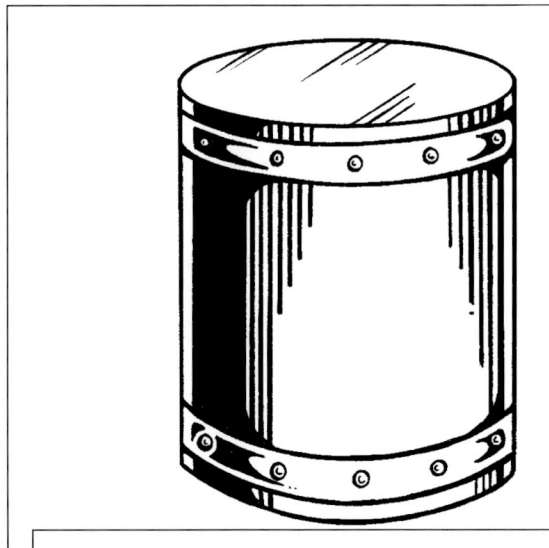

Tom-tom. This simple drum is beaten with the hand and has differing sounds or pitches.

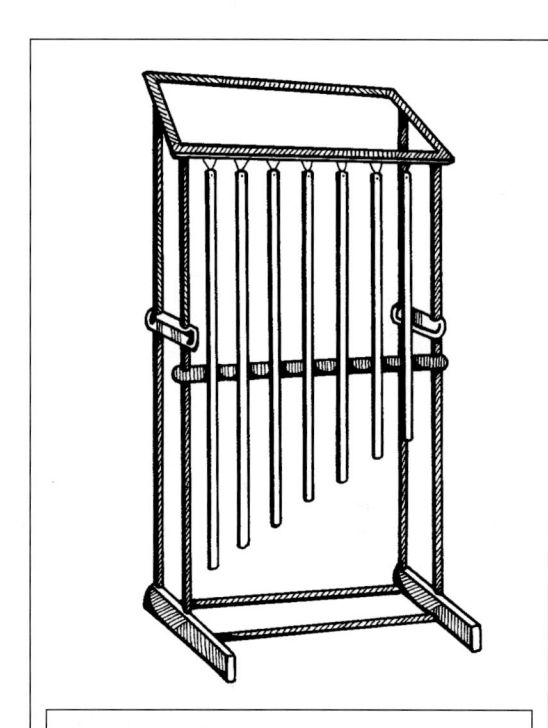

Tubular bells. This row of suspended hanging metal tubes is struck with a hammer.

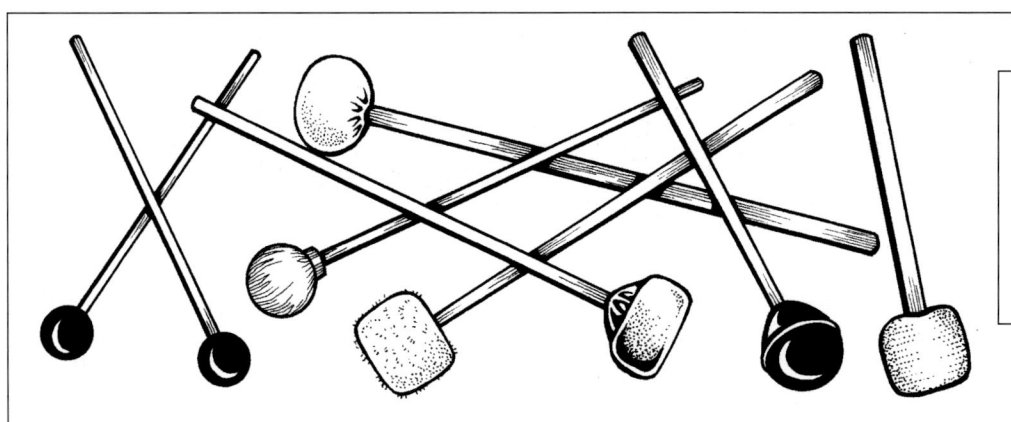

Beaters. There are many different kinds of beater – some have wooden heads while others have felt, wool or plastic heads.

Untuned percussion

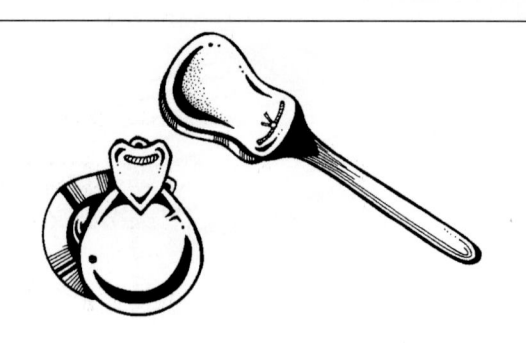

Castanets. Two hollow pieces of wood are joined together on a stick or held by the thumb and a finger. They are hit together to make a sound.

Crashing cymbals. The straps are placed around each hand and the cymbals are crashed together.
Hanging cymbal. The edge of the cymbal is tapped with a beater.

Tambour. This hand drum can be tapped with the finger-tips or hit with a beater.

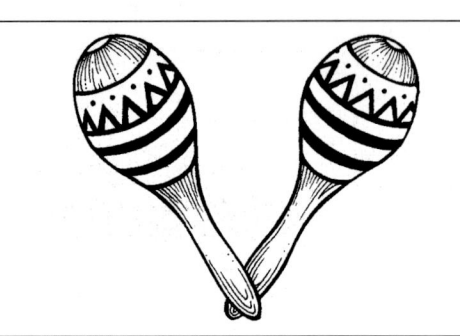

Maracas. These are shaken to produce a rattling sound.

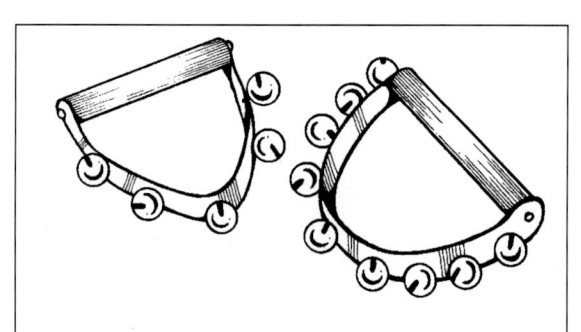

Handbells. This instrument can be shaken at random or played by tapping it with the free hand.

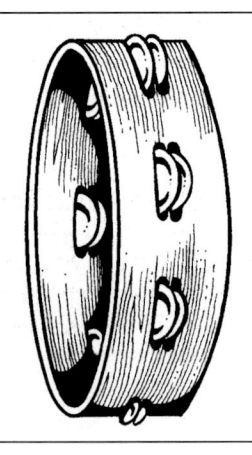

Tambourine. The metal jingles sound as the instrument is shaken or tapped.

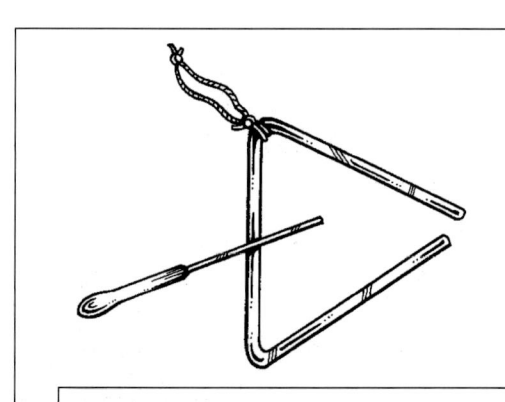

Triangle. This is held in one hand and struck with a metal beater.

Flat wood block. The block is held lightly in one hand, the beater in the other. It gives a hollow sound.
Tone block. The block is held in the middle and each side is hit with a beater to make a sound.

Cowbell. This is held in one hand and is hit with a wooden stick to give a very flat sound.

Snare drum and wire brushes. The drum has strings across one side which make a rattling sound when played with wire brushes. The other side of the drum has no strings and can be played with drumsticks.

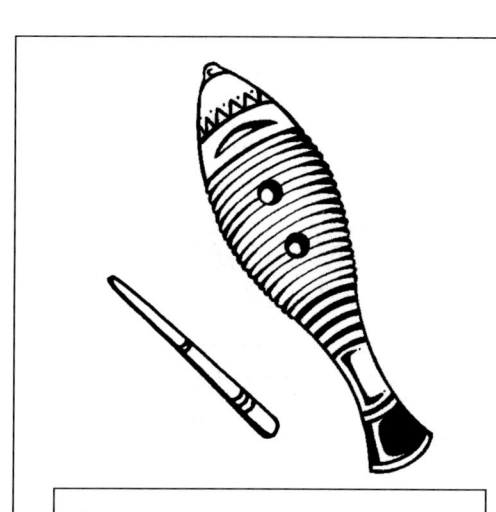

Guiro. This instrument is held on its side and a wooden stick is scraped along the ridges.

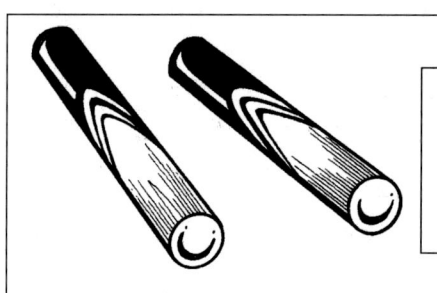

Claves. The two wooden sticks are tapped together.

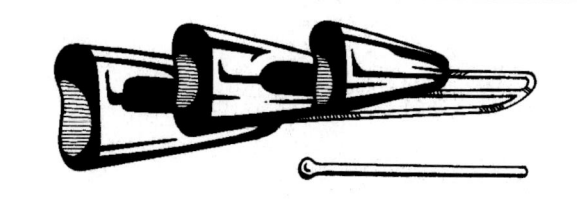

Agogo bells. This instrument is held sideways while a beater is used to tap each bell.

Rainmaker. The long tube is gently moved into an upright position to allow the seeds inside to trickle downwards.

Instruments from other countries

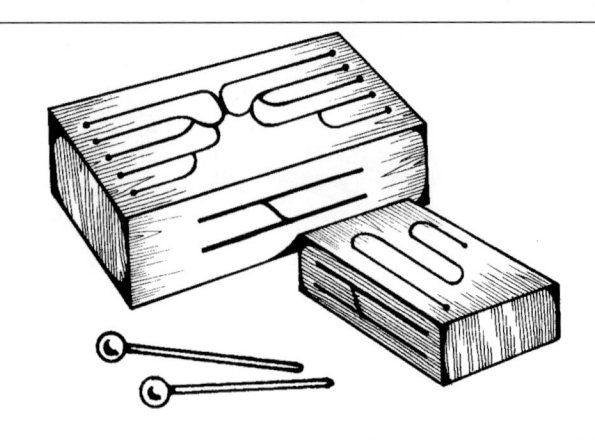

Tongue drums. These drums can produce a variety of pitched sounds unlike those of a conventional drum.

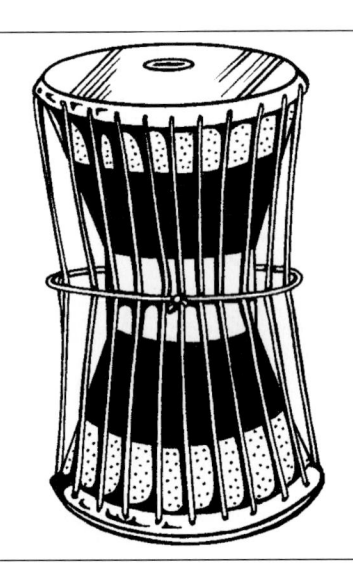

Talking drums. These have different sounds or pitches and are played with the hand.

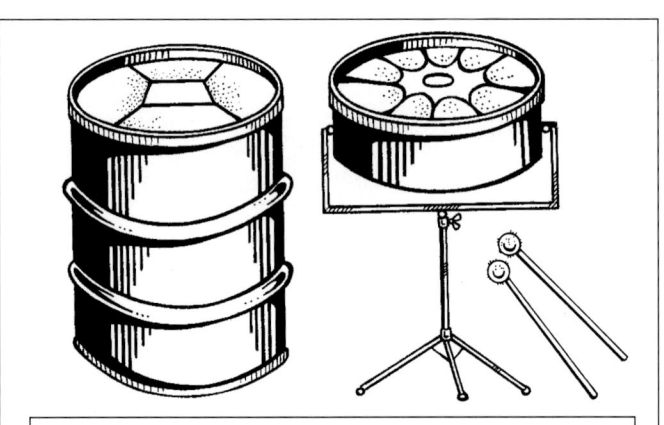

Steel drums. A Caribbean instrument. The pans were first made from the tops of oil drums and were hammered into different shapes to sound different notes.

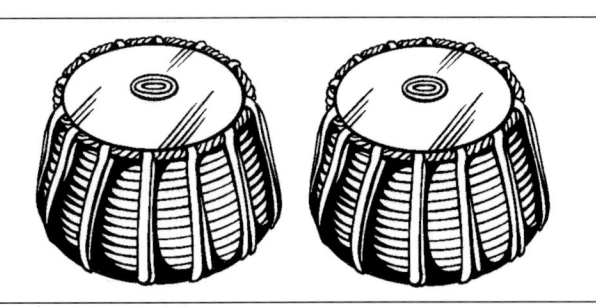

Tabla. This pair of Indian drums is played with the hands and used to accompany the sitar.

Finger cymbals. These are attached to the thumb and middle fingers and can be played to accompany dance.

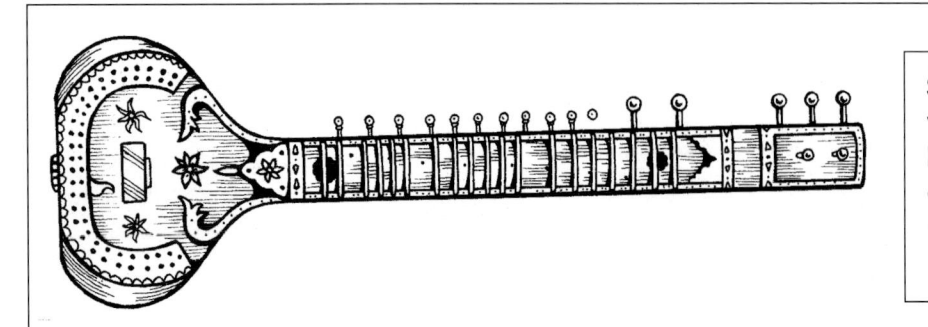

Sitar. This is a stringed instrument which belongs to the lute family. It has four strings to play the tune and three strings to play the drone (a humming background sound). It is used in Indian music.

Bongos. The bucket-shaped drums are joined together by a bar of metal and are played with the thumb and fingers.

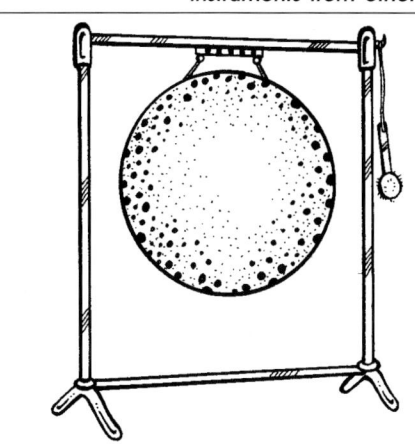

Chinese gong. This big round sheet of metal, which is turned up at the edges to form a kind of dish, is played with a soft beater.

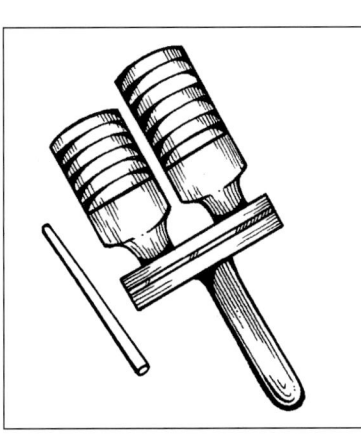

Wooden agogo. The two different sizes of hollowed wood will create interesting sounds when hit by a wide variety of beaters.

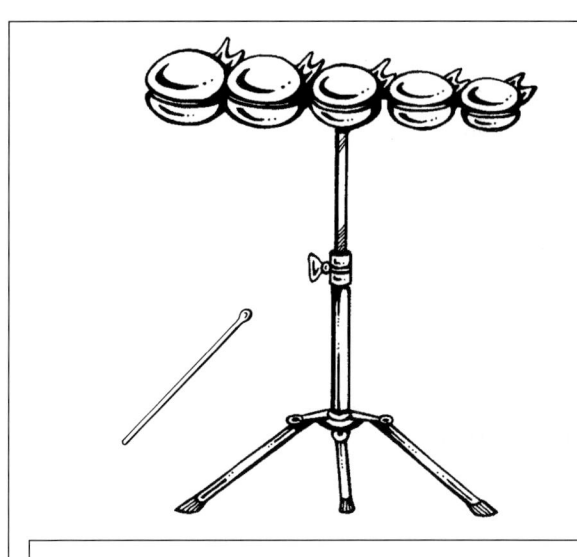

Temple blocks. These skull-shaped, hollow blocks of wood are played with a drum stick. They originated in Korea.

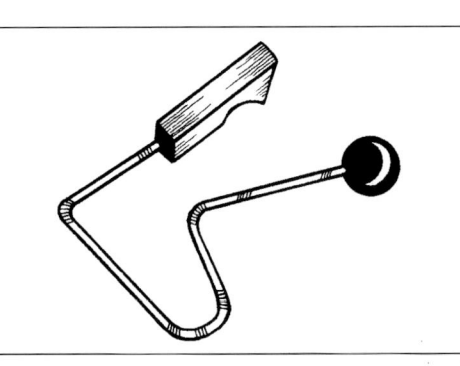

Vibraslap. This makes an effective sound when slapped against the hand.

Kalimba. This is sometimes called a thumb piano. Metal strips are fastened to a hollowed gourd or piece of wood. It is played with the thumbs.

Cabasa. This is turned back and forth on the hand to make the small metal balls sound against the drum inside.

Whistles and wind

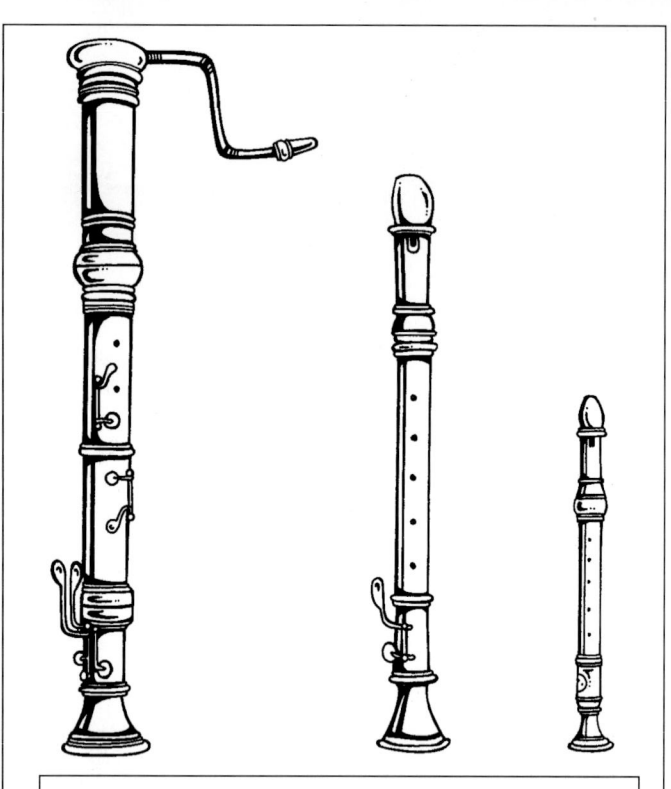

Recorders. The recorder family includes the bass, alto and descant recorders (shown here) as well as the soprano, treble and tenor recorders.

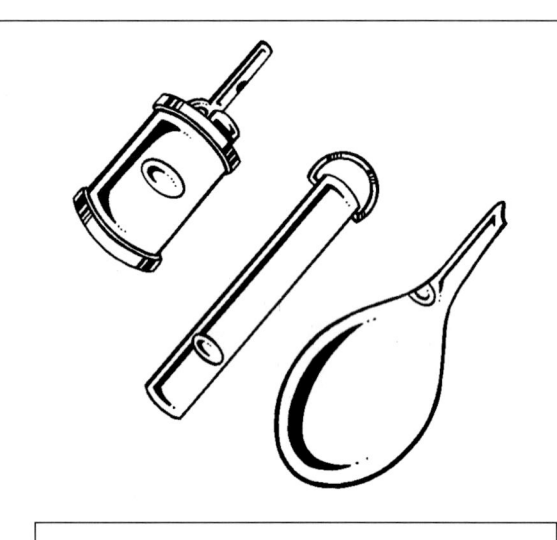

Nightingale, Duck, and Quail. These instruments imitate the sounds of birds.

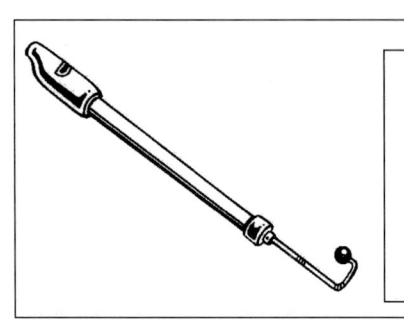

Swannee whistle. This is a slide whistle which makes high to low, and low to high sounds.

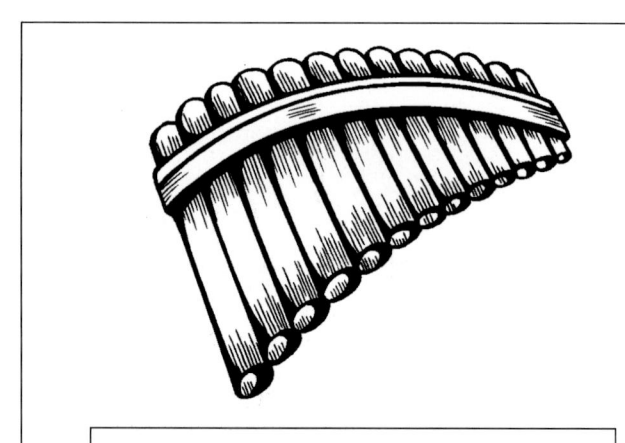

Panpipes. This is made up of a series of different sized whistles. The player blows across the open end.

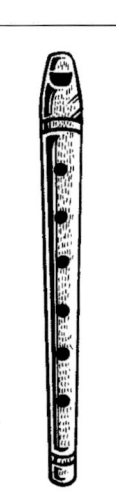

Irish pipe. This instrument is made from one piece of wood and has six holes at the front but no holes at the back.

Kazoo. Other names are 'Mirliton' or 'Tommy Talker'. The player hums or sings into the covered side hole.

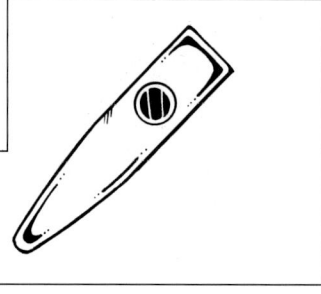

Found objects

Sand in a tray. Experiment to find ways of making the sand sound on a metal tray.

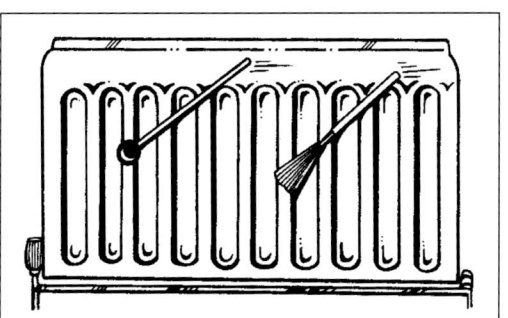

Radiator. This will make interesting sounds if a beater is dragged along the front.

Jars and cartons with seeds. These, when shaken, sound similar to maracas and rainmakers.

Spoons. The spoons can be played in many ways.

Bottles. Blow across different sized bottles to make various sounds. These sounds will change if the bottles are filled with water.

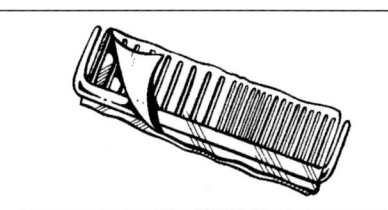

Comb and paper. Hum a tune through this.

Buckets. Upturned buckets or empty waste bins can make effective drums.

Plant pots. Different sized clay pots can be attached to strings and played like tubular bells.

Cotton reels. When strung together and shaken these make a rattling sound.

A PRIMARY TEACHER'S HANDBOOK – *Music*

flashcards

Explode

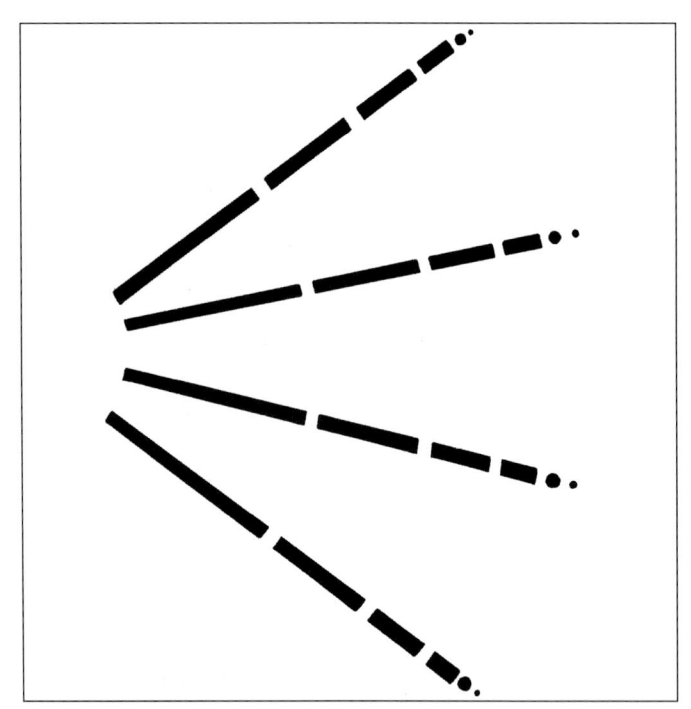

Disintegrate

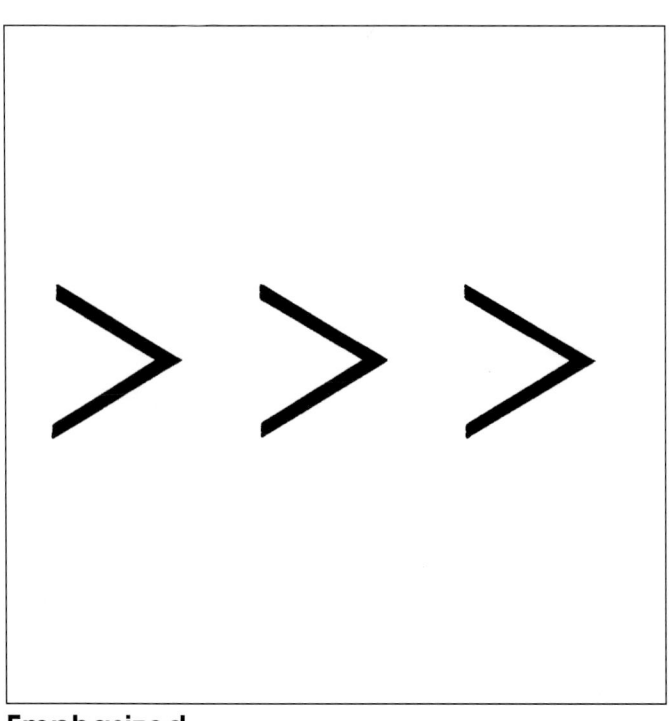

Emphasized

A PRIMARY TEACHER'S HANDBOOK – *Music*

Hiss

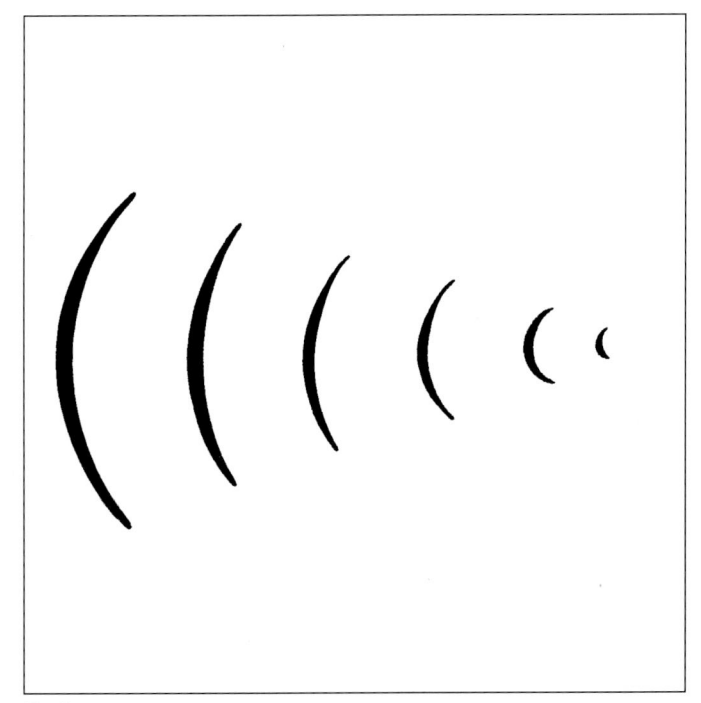

Echo

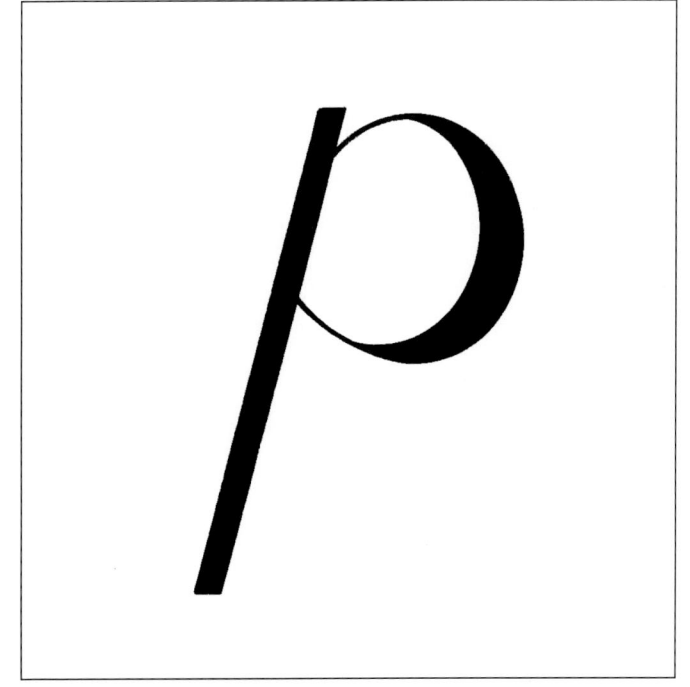

Soft

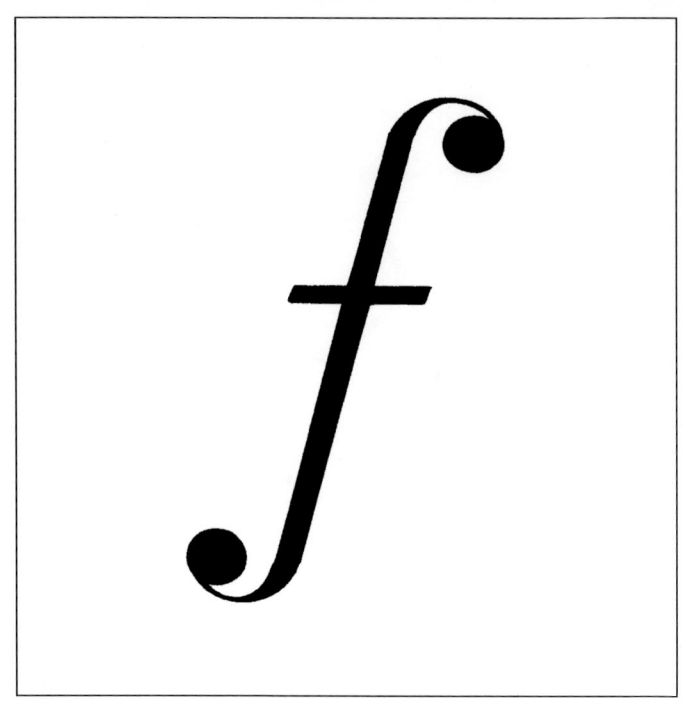

Loud

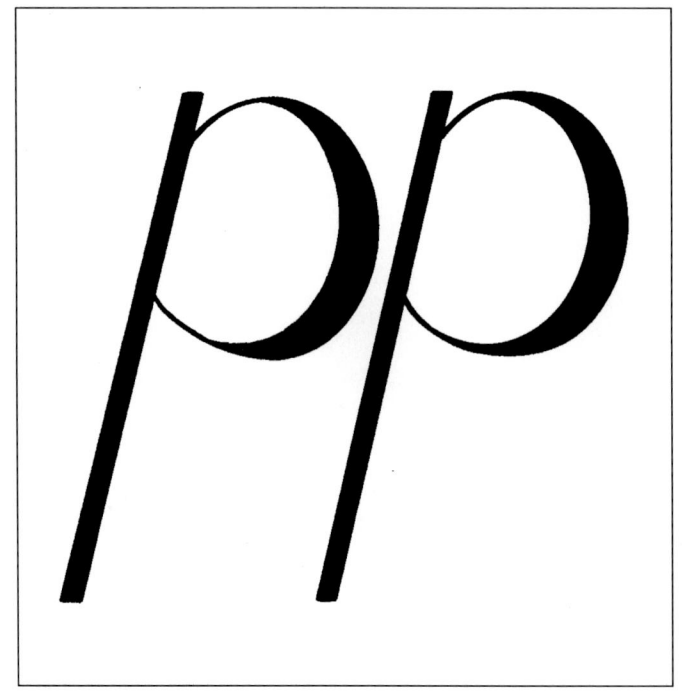

Very soft

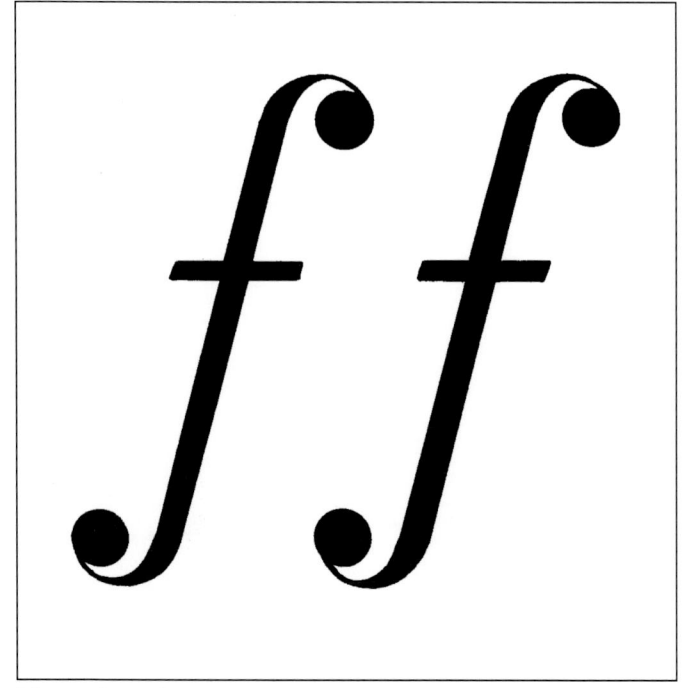

Very loud

A PRIMARY TEACHER'S HANDBOOK – *Music*

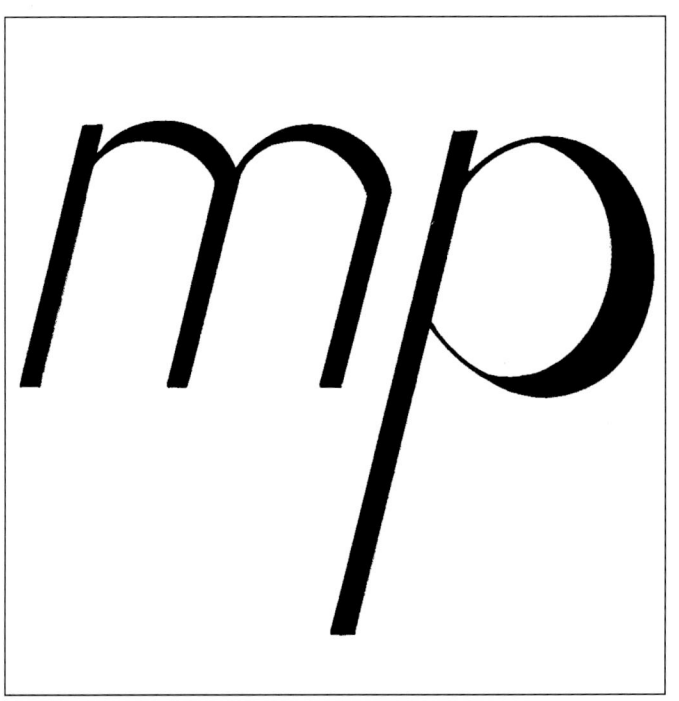

Moderately soft

Moderately loud

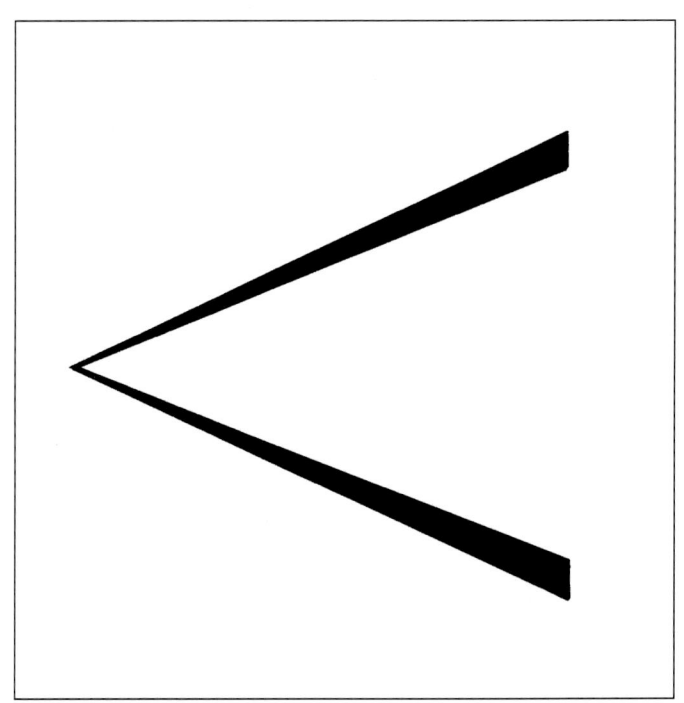

Crescendo

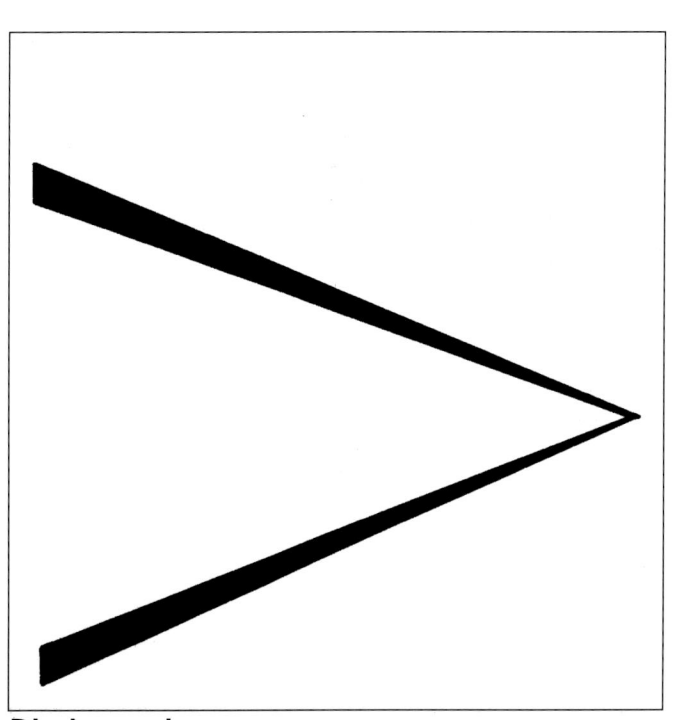

Diminuendo

Keyboard, scale and xylophone

C D E F G A B C

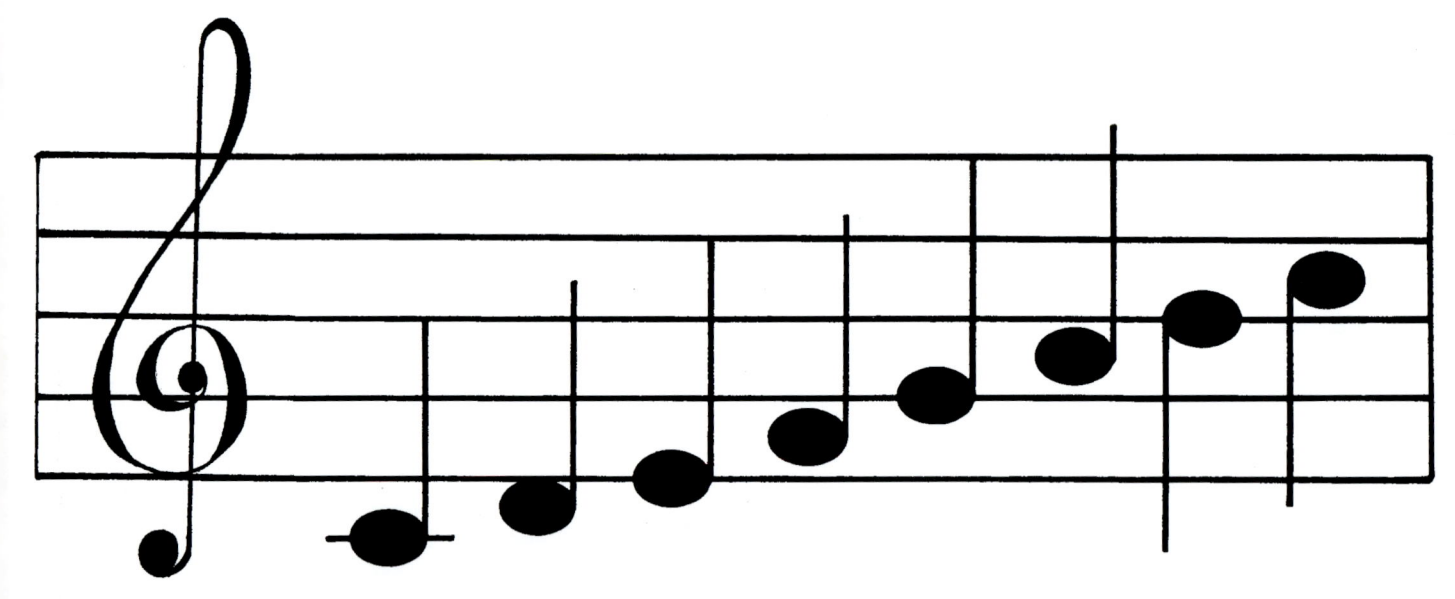

C D E F G A B C

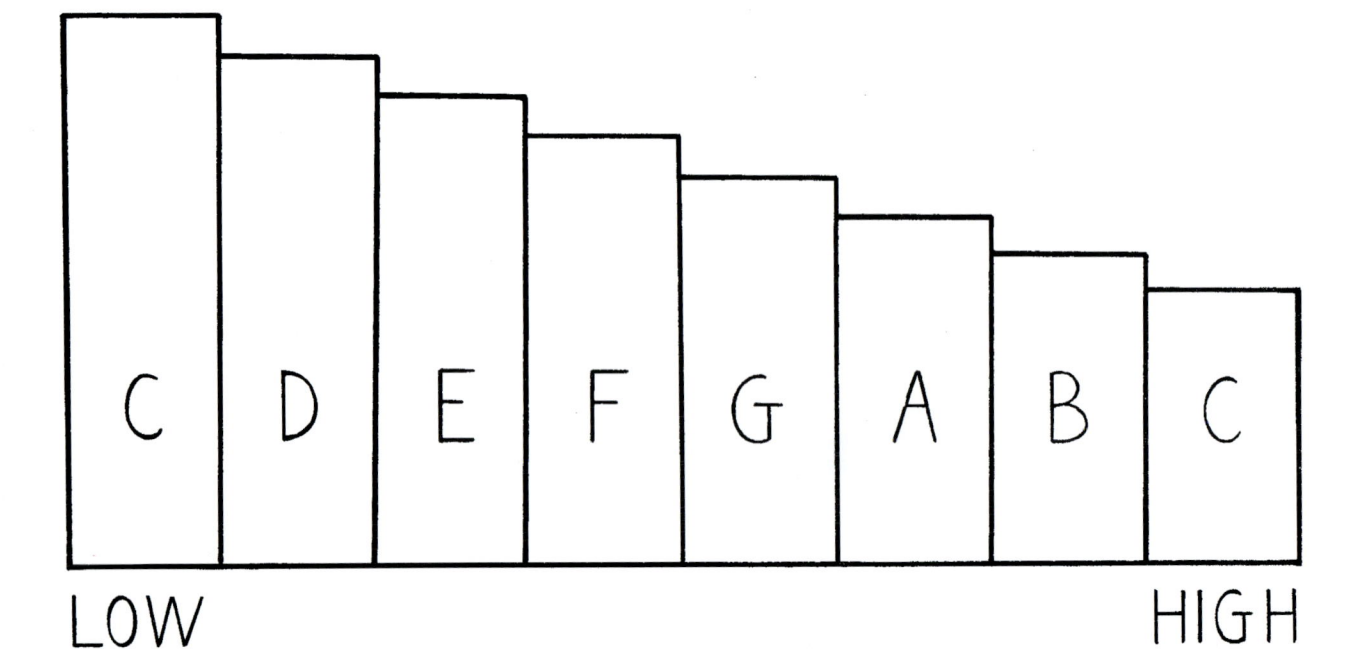

LOW   HIGH

A PRIMARY TEACHER'S HANDBOOK – *Music*

A musical score

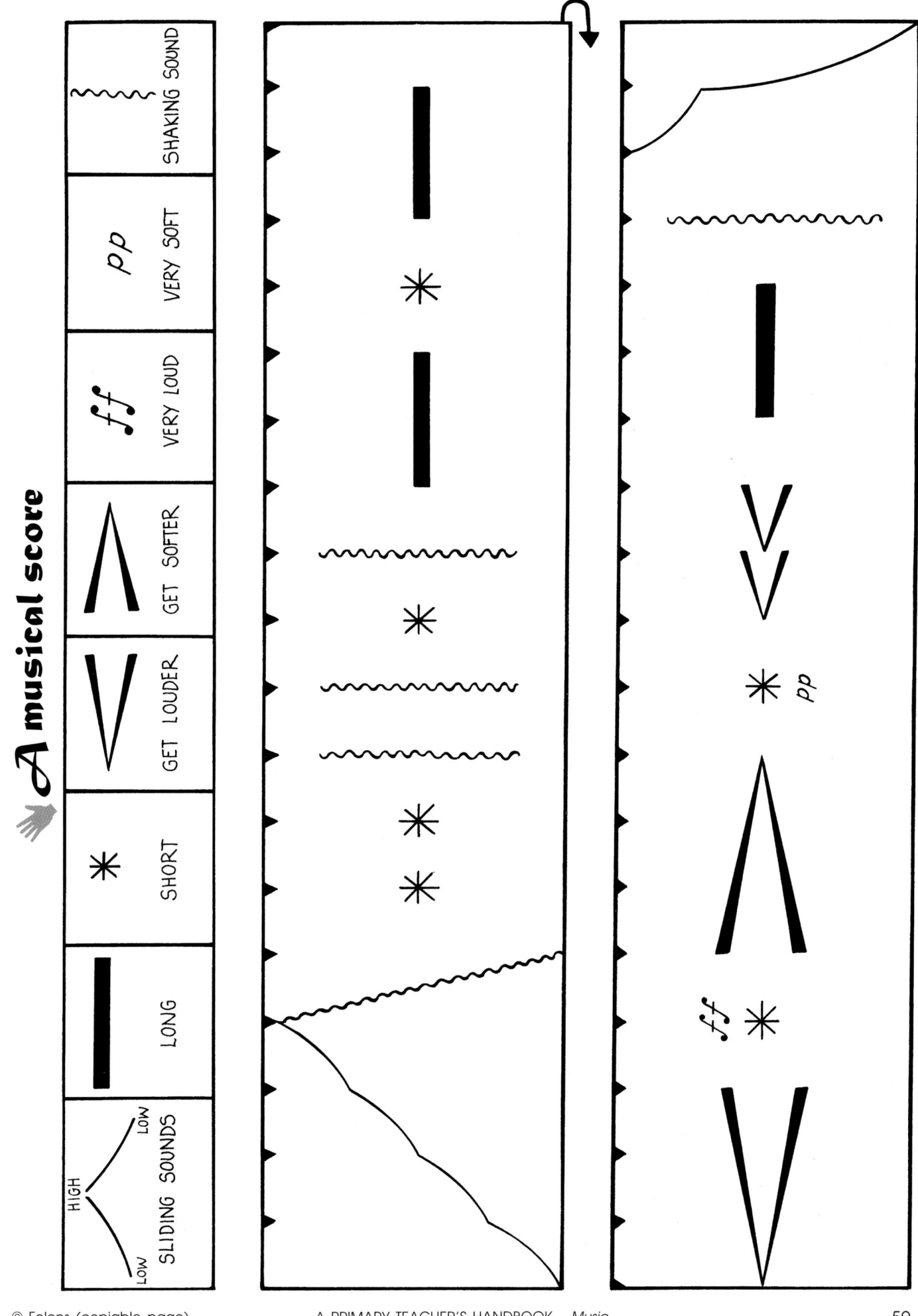

Pupil cards

It is useful to keep an up-to-date record of a child's work. The two empty pupil cards on this page are supplied as a photocopiable resource for children or teachers to fill in and keep.

Name	Year group	
Activity	**Comments**	**Date**

Name	Year group	
Activity	**Comments**	**Date**

Sound poems

Use these Sound Poems as a starting point for creative music making.

Sounds of the Seashore

Waves crashing, wind howling,
Pebbles moving, birds calling,
Sand shifting, sails flapping,
Children chattering, rocks falling.
These are sounds by the sea.

Crates clattering, cranes creaking,
Sirens sounding, lifeboats splashing,
Caves echoing, cliffs crumbling,
Fishermen shouting, ropes lashing.
Some more sounds of the sea.

Seagulls screeching, salmon leaping,
Music playing, shells crunching,
Stones plopping, seals moaning,
Donkeys braying, children munching.
Hear them all with me.

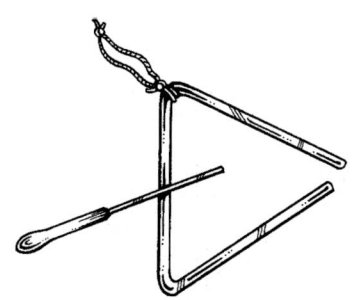

Dawn

The darkness of the sea on the edge of the night,
Clouds breaking free to let through morning light,
The sun's soft reflections sink down to the bay
And clouds gently part, letting in a new day.

The Seasons

Spring
A tip of green peeping through the soil,
The first breaking of a bud on a dark, brown branch,
Longer days.
Early morning light seeping through closed curtains,
A watery sun in a blue, blue sky,
Colour returning to gardens,
Lawn mowers on a Sunday afternoon.
The fresh smell of spring.

Summer
Long, lazy days of summer,
Blue skies, burning sun.
Children's merry laughter,
Distant chimes of an ice-cream van,
Tractors chugging through golden fields,
Buzzing wasps,
Fluttering butterflies.
Long, hot, summer.

Autumn
Damp,
Cold, wet, damp.
Fallen leaves underfoot –
Red, gold, yellow, brown.
Crackling bonfires,
Sparking fireworks,
Curling smoke.
Damp, wet, autumn.

Winter
Cold, dark, long nights,
Frost sparkling on frozen glass,
White snow, falling softly,
Church bells chiming across the silent night,
Families chattering around a crackling fire.
Sharp, cold winter.

Music spinner

Cut out the hexagon below and mount it on card. Push a matchstick through the middle to make a music spinner.

Suggested instruments

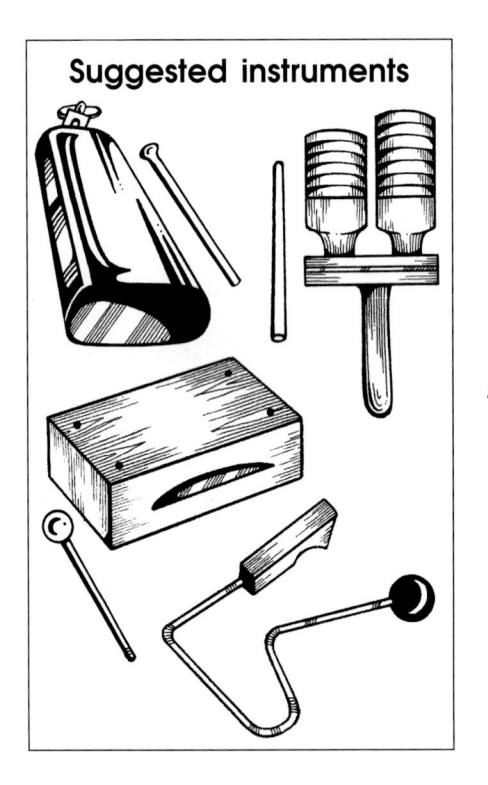

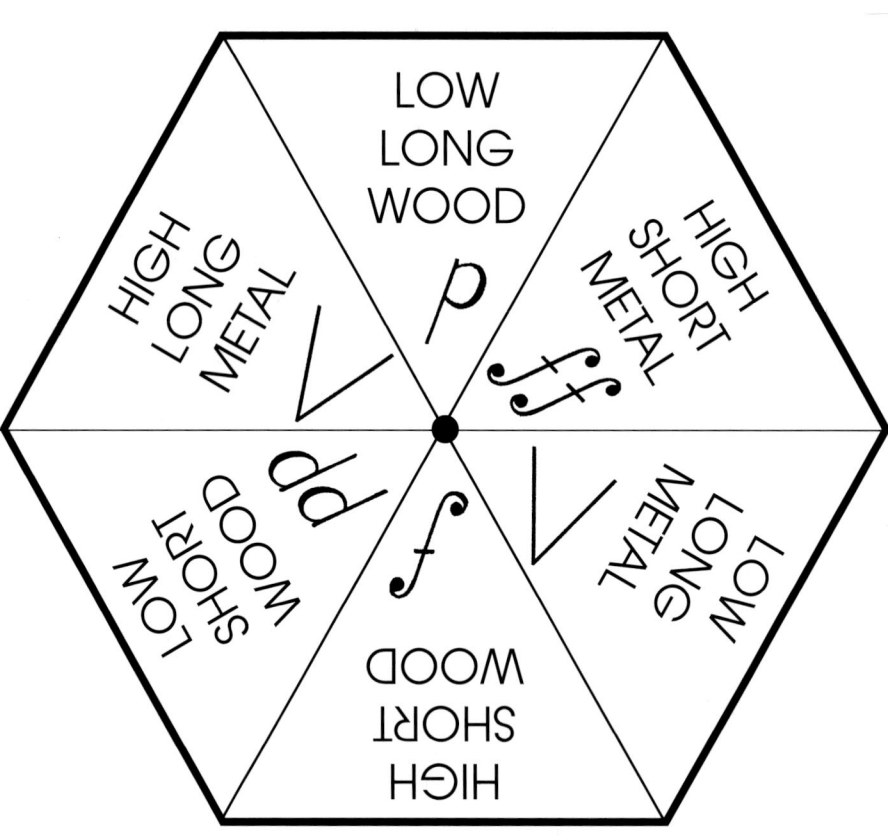

Spinner segments:
LOW LONG WOOD — p
HIGH SHORT METAL — ff
LOW LONG METAL — v
HIGH SHORT WOOD — f
LOW SHORT WOOD — pp
HIGH LONG METAL — v

- Spin your music spinner six times.
- Record your results in the table below.
- Follow the table and perform the piece of music on instruments of your choice.

A	B	C
D	E	F

A PRIMARY TEACHER'S HANDBOOK – *Music*

Useful resources

The information below is correct at the time of going to print.

Books

Bright Ideas
Richard Addison (Scholastic).

Gently into Music
Mary York (Longman).
Ready-planned music lessons.

Exploring Sound
June Tillman (Stainer & Bell).

High Low Dolly Pepper
Veronica Clark (A & C Black).

Key Ideas Music
Christine Richards (Folens).

Musical Allsorts
John Wilson and Charles Rosamond (OUP).
Graded music topics for KS2.

Music All The Time (Bks 1 & 2)
Wendy Bird and Elizabeth Bennett (J & W Chester).

Music and Magic
Alan Blackwood (OUP).
A guide to using taped music.

Music Through Topics: for Infants
Veronica Clark (CUP).

Pompaleerie Jig
Kate Baxter and Diana Thompson (Nelson).
A collection of musical games.

Story, Song and Dance
Jean Gilbert (CUP).

Three Singing Pigs
Kaye Umansky (A & C Black).

Word Games, More Word Games
Sandy Brownjohn and Janet Whitaker (Hodder and Stoughton).

Songbooks

Alleluya
chosen by David Gadsby and John Hoggarth (A & C Black).

Apusskidu
chosen by Beatrice Harrop, Peggy Blakely and David Gadsby (A & C Black).

Birds and Beasts
chosen by Sheena Roberts (A & C Black).

Boomps-a-daisy
(A & C Black).

Carol, Gaily Carol
chosen by Beatrice Harrop (A & C Black).

Count me in
(A & C Black).

Every Colour Under the Sun
(Ward Lock Educational).

Flying a Round
chosen by David Gadsby and Beatrice Harrop (A & C Black).

Game Songs with Prof Dogg's Troupe
chosen by Harriet Powell (A & C Black).

Harlequin
chosen by David Gadsby and Beatrice Harrop (A & C Black).

Hullabaloo-balay!
Barrie Turner (Nelson).

The Jolly Herring
chosen by Roger Bush (A & C Black).

Juke Box
(A & C Black).

Kokoleoko
(Music Sales).

Merrily to Bethlehem
chosen by David Gadsby and Ivor Golby (A & C Black).

Mrs Macaroni
June Tillman (Nelson).

Musical Calendar of Festivals
chosen by Barbara Cass-Beggs (Ward Lock Educational).

Okki-tokki-unga
Beatrice Harrop, Linda Friend and David Gadsby (A & C Black).

Phantasmagoria
Kaye Umansky (A & C Black).

Sing a Song for fun/celebration
Martin Stumble (Cassell).

Sing a Story
Graham Westcott (A & C Black).

Sing for Your Life
chosen by Sandra Kerr (A & C Black).

The Singing Sack
compiled by Helen East (A & C Black).

Sing 'n' Learn
Chris Bolton (Sing 'n' Learn Publications).

Someone's Singing, Lord
chosen by Beatrice Harrop (A & C Black).

Strawberry Fair
(A & C Black).

Ta-ra-ra Boom-de-ay
chosen by David Gadsby and Beatrice Harrop (A & C Black).

Tinder-box
chosen by by Sylvia Barratt and Sheena Hodge (A & C Black).

Whoopsey Diddledy Dandy Dee
Shirley Winfield and Diana Thompson (Universal Edition).

Useful addresses

The Disabled Living Foundation
380/384 Harrow Road, London W9 2HU. Tel: 0171 2896111

Knock on Wood
Global Music Supplies, Arch X, Granary Wharf, Leeds LS1 4BR.
Tel: 0113 242 9146

Percussion Plus
Ludlow Hill Road, West Bridgford, Nottingham NG2 6HD
Tel: 0115 936 0450

The Royal College of Music
Prince Consort Road, South Kensington, London SW7 2BS.
Tel: 0171 5893643

Glossary of terminology

Acoustic instrument
An instrument on which the sound created by the player is the sound that is heard – not electronic.

Bass clef
The sign which is found at the beginning of music to indicate low sounding voices or instruments. It looks like:

Binary form
A piece of music in this form has two different parts – A and B.

Canon
A piece of music where the main tune is imitated by different parts.

Chord
More than one note playing at the same time.

Common time
Another name for 4/4 time: four crotchet beats in a bar.

Crescendo
The sign that means getting louder. It looks like: <

Diatonic scales
The scales of the major and minor keys.

Diminuendo
The sign that means getting softer. It looks like: >

Duration
The length of time that something lasts (long, short, beat, rhythm).

Dynamics
Different levels of volume.

Electronic
The instrument has no strings or pipes. The sound is produced electrically.

Elements
This means pitch/duration/dynamics/tempo/timbre/texture. These are used within a structured piece of music.

Forte
The sound is strong or loud. It looks like: f

Improvise
To create at will.

Key signature
The sharps or the flats seen at the beginning of a piece of music telling the performer in which key to perform.

Legato
Formed without breaks between notes. The sign to indicate this is:

Metronome
A mechanical device which fixes the tempo/speed of a piece.

Notation – graphic, traditional
A way in which a composer writes down music. Graphic notation in the classroom uses symbols created by the children. Traditional notation has been used in the western world for generations.

Ostinato/drone
A tune that repeats itself.

Pentatonic
A five-note scale (eg the white notes of the piano leaving out the Fs and Bs).

Phrasing
The division of music into different sections. These sections often occur naturally and are called phrases.

Piano
The sign which means soft. It looks like: p

Pitch
High and low sounds.

Pizzicato
Short/plucked notes.

Rondo
A piece of music in which a tune recurs. It could be: ABACADA.

Round
A short canon that is sung. The same tune is sung by different voices at different times.

Score
A music copy that shows the whole of the piece of music.

Staccato
Formed with short, detached notes. The sign to indicate this looks like:

Structure
Different ways in which sounds are organised.

Tempo
Different speeds.

Ternary form
This form of music has a sandwich look 'ABA'.

Texture
Different ways in which sounds are put together.

Timbre
Different qualities of sound – harsh, mellow, hollow, bright.

Time signature
The numbers at the beginning of a piece of music which indicate how many beats there are in each bar.

Treble clef
The sign at the beginning of music for high voices/instruments. It looks like:

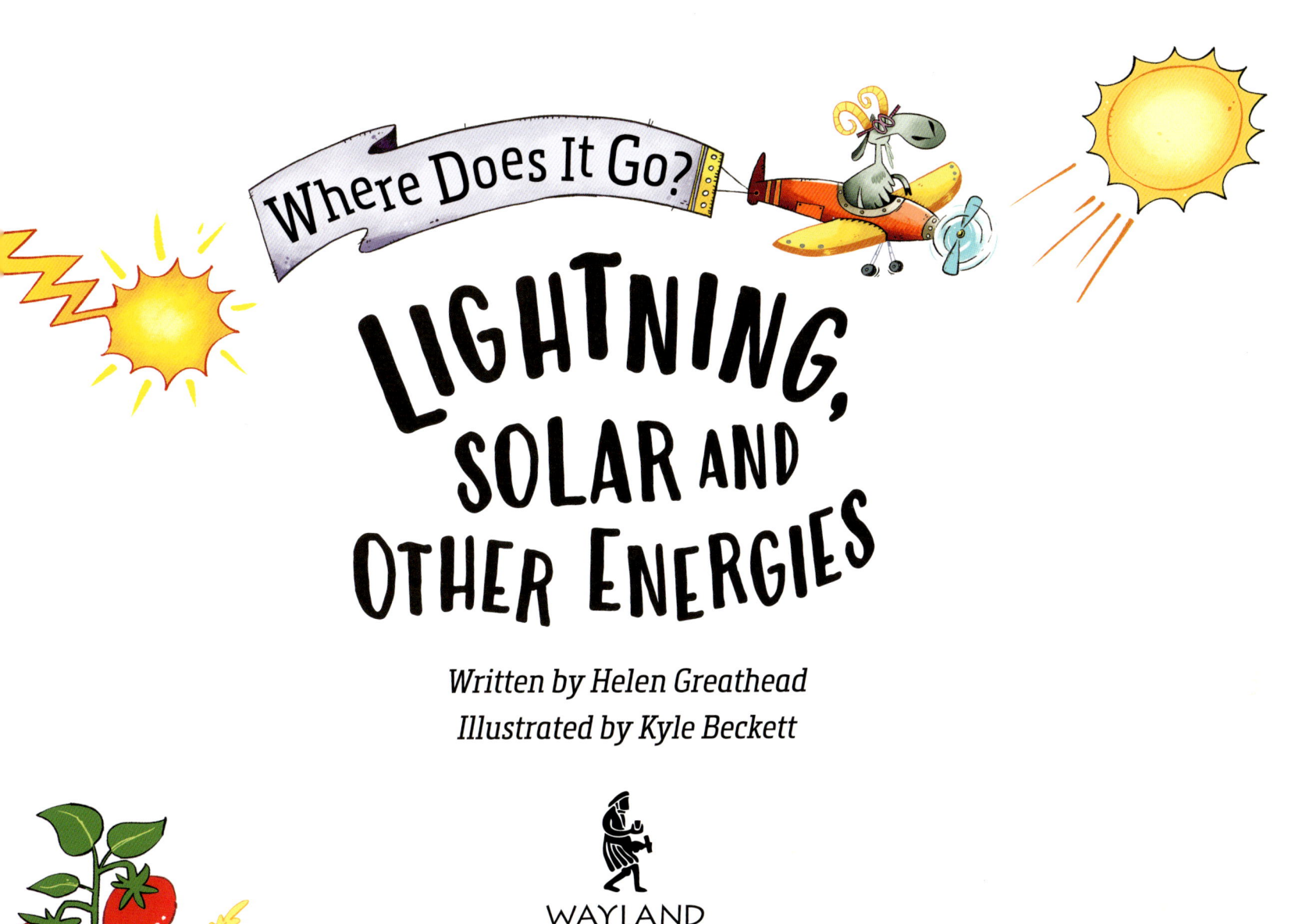

Where Does It Go?

LIGHTNING, SOLAR AND OTHER ENERGIES

Written by Helen Greathead

Illustrated by Kyle Beckett

WAYLAND

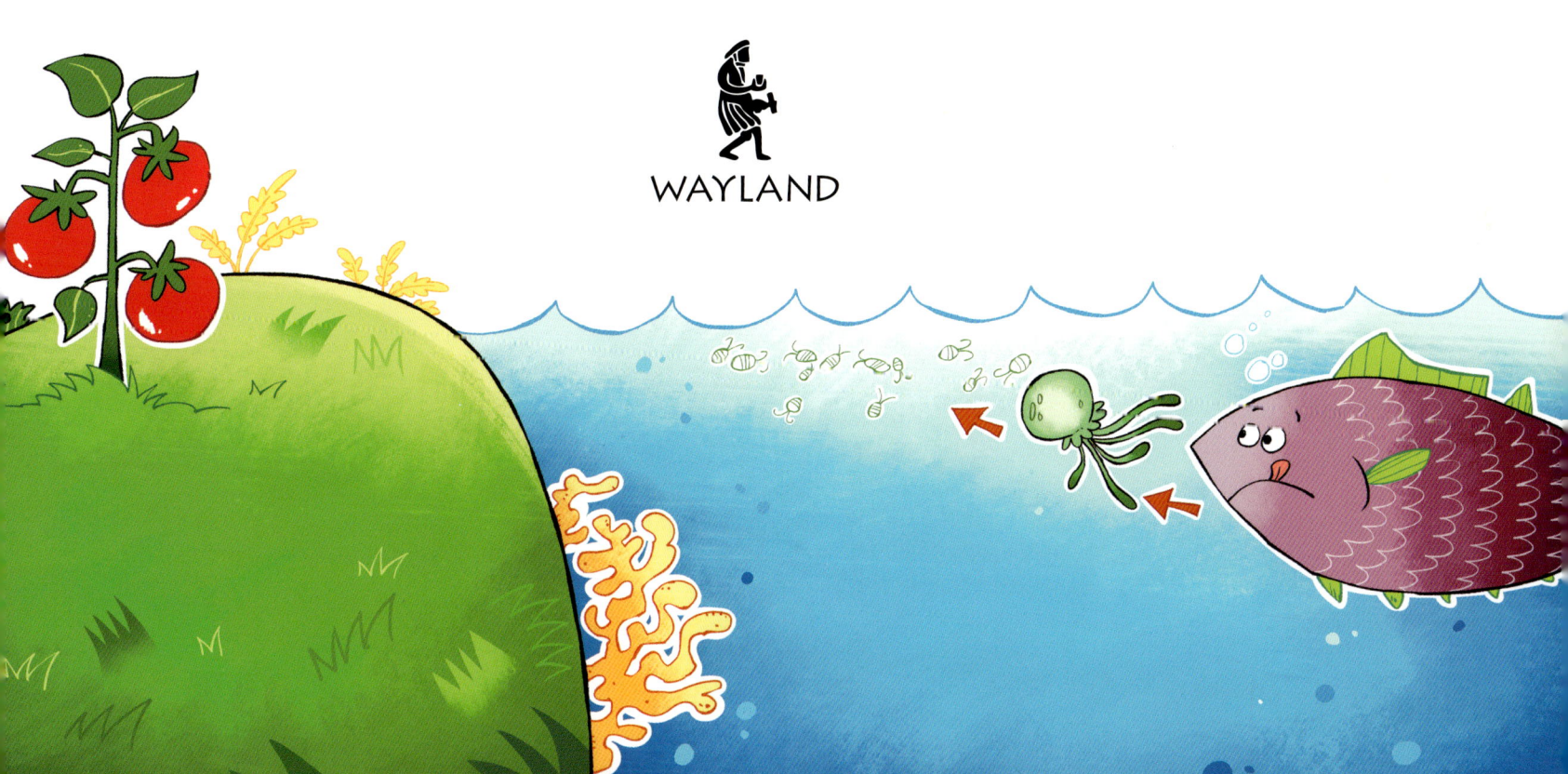

First published in Great Britain in 2023
by Wayland

Copyright © Hodder and Stoughton Ltd, 2023

All rights reserved

Commissioning Editor: Elise Short
Editor: Nicola Edwards

Designers: Anthony Hannant and Gemma Steward

ISBN: 978 1 5263 2269 2 HB

ISBN: 978 1 5263 2270 8 PB

10 9 8 7 6 5 4 3 2 1

Wayland, an imprint of
Hachette Children's Group

Part of Hodder and Stoughton

Carmelite House
50 Victoria Embankment
London EC4Y 0DZ

An Hachette UK Company

www.hachette.co.uk

www.hachettechildrens.co.uk

Printed and bound in Dubai

MIX
Paper from
responsible sources
FSC® C104740

CONTENTS

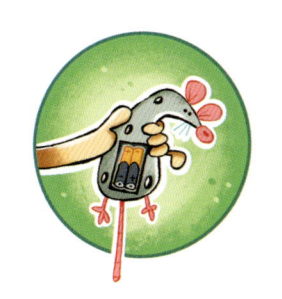

WHAT ON EARTH IS ENERGY?

We can't usually see it, but we need it for just about everything we do! Energy comes in lots of different forms. In this book we'll find out how these different types of energy provide the power to let things move, work and grow. And we'll find out where that energy goes when we've used it.

These are just a few forms of energy and some of the things they can do:

Heat energy keeps us warm.

Heat energy cooks our food.

Chemical energy creates a reaction that allows fire to burn.

Light energy helps us to see in the dark.

Sound energy lets us hear things.

NOOO-my hot dog!

4

Energy doesn't always stay the same. It can change from one type to another.

As the hot dog falls from the bun, it uses **kinetic** energy.

Kinetic energy makes things move.

Kinetic energy turns to **heat** energy when it hits the ground.

Electrical energy comes from a power station.

1. **Heat** energy, for example from coal, boils water to produce steam.

2. The steam turns a turbine, which powers a generator that is made up of magnets and wires.

Electrons travel along cables.

Generator

Turbine

Heat energy becomes **kinetic** energy.

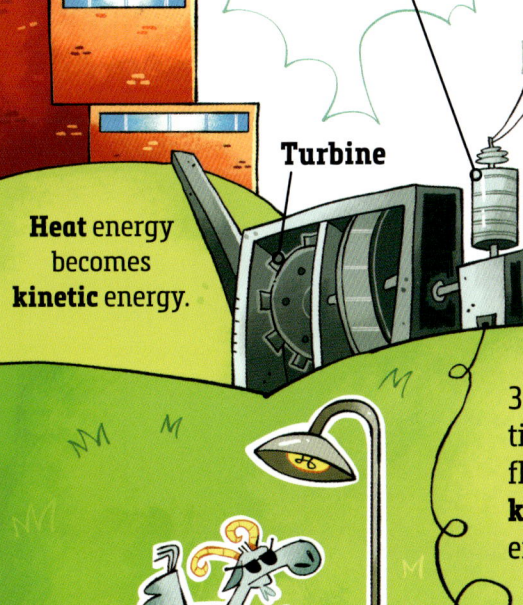

3. When the generator moves, tiny particles, called electrons, flow through the wires, turning **kinetic** energy into **electrical** energy that's sent to our homes.

The fuel that supplied the power station was an energy store. We can also say it's '**potential** energy', because we know it could provide energy even though it isn't at the moment.

So how is energy stored? And what is **potential** energy?

GET MOVING

Can you guess what this battery and this log have in common?

Battery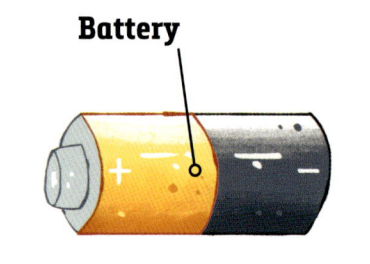

Wooden log

Believe it or not, they're both storing energy!

The battery stores chemical energy. That chemical energy can convert into kinetic energy, then electrical energy.

Chemical energy store

Electrical and mechanical energy make the toy move.

The lump of wood also stores chemical energy.

The chemical energy can convert into heat and light energy.

A force called gravity made this log fall.

Gravity is a force that pulls objects towards the centre of Earth.

Before the log fell to the ground, it was storing what's called 'gravitational potential energy'. Gravitational potential energy just means that because the log was quite high off the ground, there was a possibility that it could move with the help of gravity.

Gravitational potential energy

When the log fell, and started moving, the potential energy turned into kinetic energy.

Here's another example of gravitational potential energy turning into kinetic energy. Check out these skateboarders jumping off a half-pipe:

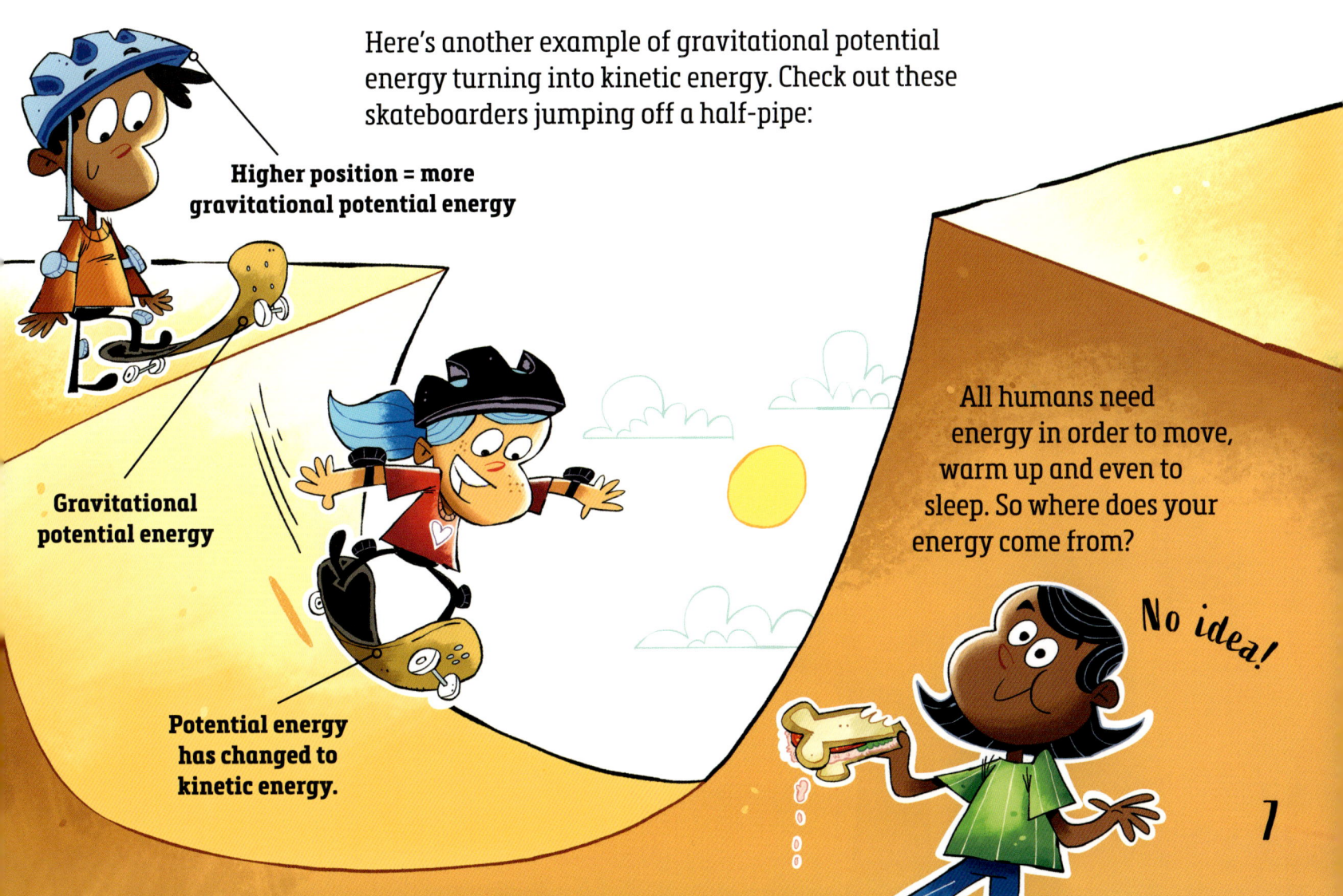

Higher position = more gravitational potential energy

Gravitational potential energy

Potential energy has changed to kinetic energy.

All humans need energy in order to move, warm up and even to sleep. So where does your energy come from?

No idea!

7

YOU'VE GOT THE POWER

You and all humans get energy from food.

Yes, the food and water we put in our bodies contain the energy that makes our bodies work. From breathing to running marathons, everything we do needs energy.

Some foods provide more energy than others:

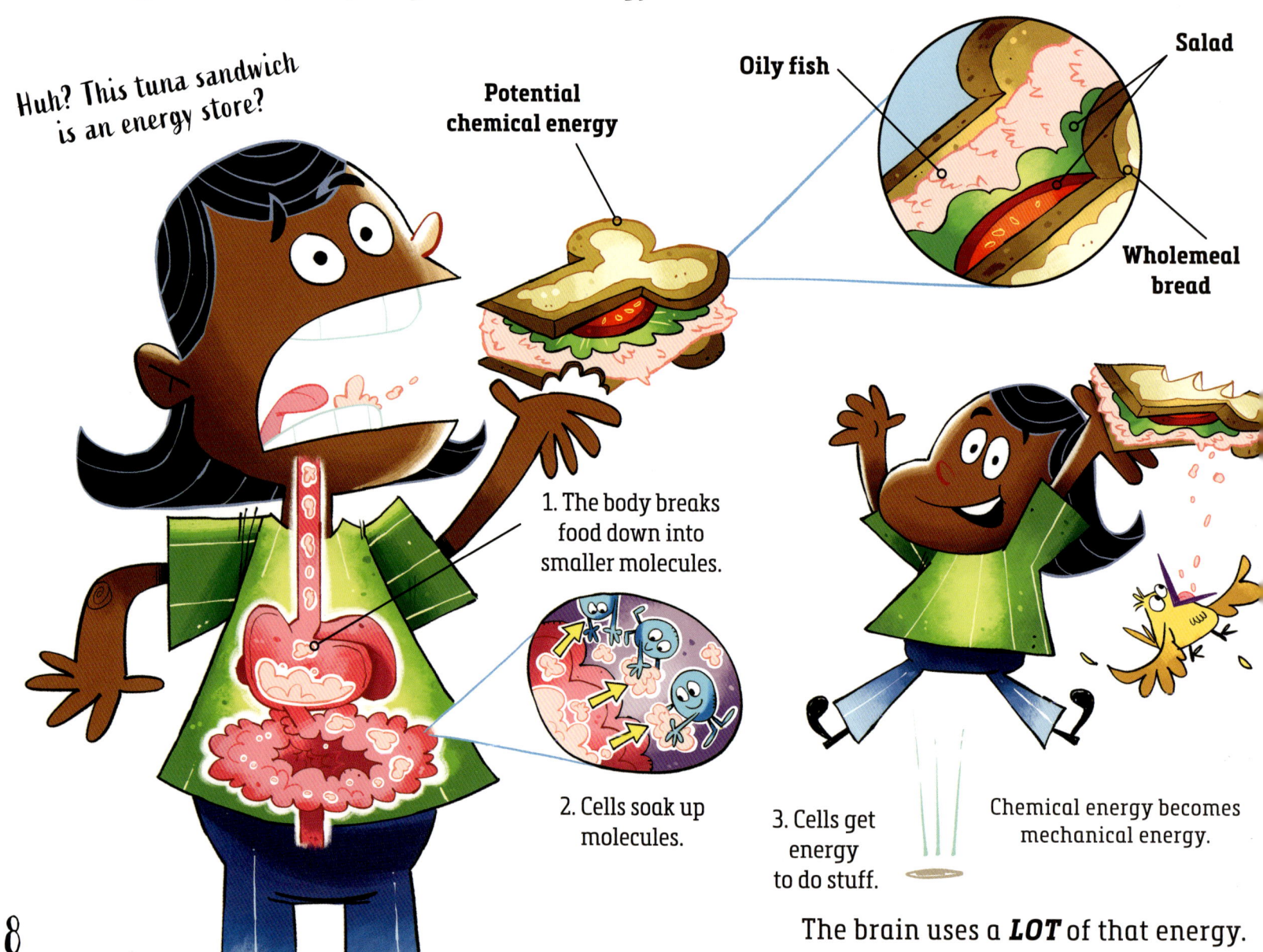

Oily fish

Salad

Wholemeal bread

Huh? This tuna sandwich is an energy store?

Potential chemical energy

1. The body breaks food down into smaller molecules.

2. Cells soak up molecules.

3. Cells get energy to do stuff.

Chemical energy becomes mechanical energy.

The brain uses a **LOT** of that energy.

8

A network of neurons

There are **around 86 billion** cells – called neurons – in your brain, which is where your body's decisions are made. Chemical energy converts to electrical energy to send signals pinging from one neuron to the next and instructions along nerves in the body.

Did you know ...
There's enough electrical energy in a human brain to power a light bulb.

This looks bad!

It is bad! Move feet! RUN!

Brain signals travel at speeds up to **320 kph**.

From Sun to sandwich

So where did the energy in your sandwich come from? Animals (including us humans) get their energy from eating plants and other animals. Plants get their energy from the Sun.

Light energy

Tomatoes

Lettuce

Wheat

Plankton

Tuna

Jellyfish

Potential chemical energy

Potential energy

In fact, most energy on Earth comes from the Sun ...

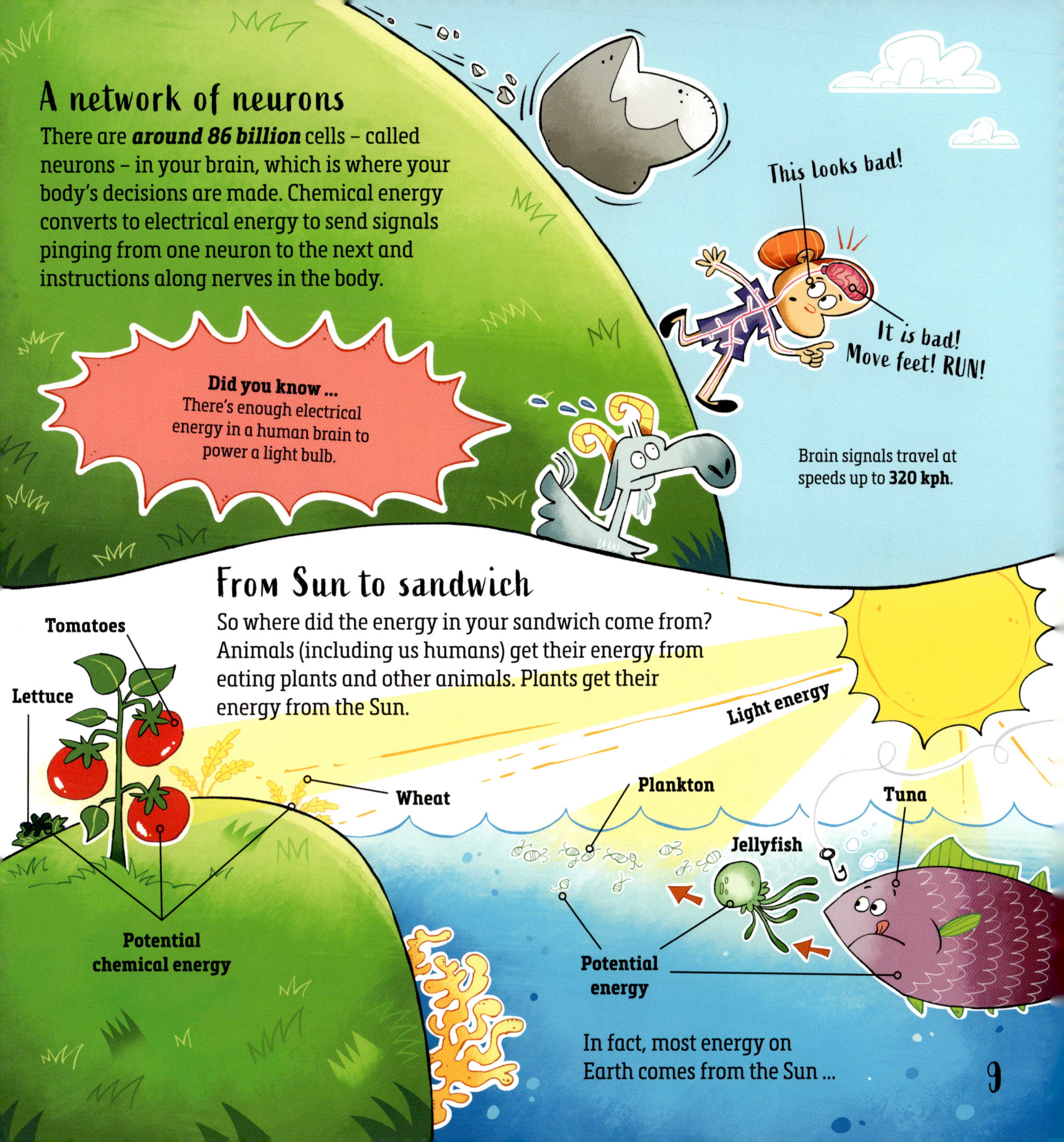

9

SUNSATIONAL

The Sun, our nearest star, is actually **150 million km** away! It's made up of hydrogen and helium gases. There would be no life on Earth without it. But luckily, our planet is in the right position to make use of the Sun's heat and light energy.

It takes *8 minutes and 20 seconds* for the Sun's rays to reach Earth.

The Sun releases **4.26 million tonnes** of energy per second!

Extracting energy

All plants, including plant plankton in the sea, use sunlight to create energy that they store as sugar. They do this through a process called photosynthesis.

Gives off oxygen

Soaks up carbon dioxide (CO_2)

Produces sugars (potential chemical energy)

Water

Animals that eat plants get energy from the sugars, too. Animals that eat plant-eating animals also get energy from those sugars.

Uh-oh!

Yum!

People were using the Sun's energy for warmth and light long before there was an electricity supply.

- They got up at sunrise and went to bed at sunset.
- They dried food in the sun to make it last longer.
- They evaporated seawater to produce salt.

Six thousand years ago, some Chinese communities designed houses that used the Sun's heat and light energy. Architects today use some of the same ideas to design houses that stay cool in summer and warm in winter.

The roof provides shade against the hot Sun.

Windows let in the Sun's warmth in winter.

But what did people do when the Sun went down?

Humans have probably been warming themselves around fires for probably **over 700,000 years** – ever since they realised that they could extract the heat and light energy stored in wood, straw, seaweed and animal poo.

How did people know about fires? Maybe lightning showed them what it could do ...

STRIKE A LIGHT

Imagine seeing lightning for the first time and not knowing what it was.

Lightning causes wildfires that destroy forests and wildlife. But it also creates heat and clears land. This made hunting and foraging for food easier for humans thousands of years ago. Some experts believe it taught people that cooked food tasted good.

As the planet gets hotter (see page 17), warmer air is causing more thunderstorms. When lightning strikes a tree, it can burn easily. Other trees quickly catch fire until a whole forest can be ablaze. These wildfires are hard to control.

But where does lightning come from?

It begins in a thundercloud.

Thundercloud

Ice crystal

Moisture molecule

Positive charge

Negative charge

1. Billions of cold ice crystals and warm moisture molecules rub together in the cloud.

2. They create static electricity (the stuff that makes your hair stand on end when you take off a jumper).

3. Just like a battery, the electricity has positive and negative charges.

4. Increasing negative charges send an electric current racing towards the ground.

5. Positive charges from tall objects or the ground rise up to meet the current.

6. Lightning flashes until the negative charges are used up.

Did you know ...
The temperature around a lightning flash can be *five times* as hot as the Sun's surface.

Did you know ...
There are *50-100* lightning strikes per second around the world today.

Could we catch the electricity from a lightning bolt?

13

SKY POWER

One bolt of lightning holds enough energy to toast **100,000** slices of bread!

In 2013, researchers at Southampton University, UK, created a fake lightning bolt. They used it to charge a mobile phone battery.

Perhaps we COULD power our homes with energy from lightning? Well, one company tried to make it happen in 2007. They soon gave up.

The trouble is, lightning ...

... happens too fast

... is too random – we never know where it will strike next!

Electrical potential energy from a storm cloud changes into light energy (the flash you see in the sky) and sound energy (the thunderclap you hear), but most of it becomes heat energy. A lightning flash can heat the air surrounding it to **39,000 °C** in a fraction of a second, but that heat is absorbed quickly into the atmosphere.

Did you know ...
Ball lightning is, well, ball-shaped. It might be as small as a pea, or big as a car. It lasts up to 20 seconds and can hover in the air, roll along the ground, or crash into people's homes!

... doesn't always hit the ground

... loses more energy as it gets closer to Earth.

Lightning's energy is practically impossible to capture, but there are easier ways to get power ...

PREHISTORIC POWER

Today, over 60 per cent of the energy we use for heating, lighting and to power machines comes from coal, oil and natural gas. We call these 'fossil fuels' because they're the remains of animals and plants that died millions of years ago. Earth looked very different then.

Swampy forests

Plankton

Shallow seas

How fossil fuels are made:

Dead animals sink

This took millions of years.

Covered with mud and sediment

Sediment turns to rock.

Dead plants sink

Squashed by heat and pressure from above

Buried

Dead plants turn to coal.

Dead algae and animals turn to oil and gas.

Natural gas

Oil

Natural gas makes electricity and heats homes.

Oil makes electricity and fuels transport.

The problem with fossil fuels

When prehistoric plants and animals died, the CO_2 inside them was buried in the ground. Burning fossil fuels releases this ancient CO_2 into the atmosphere again – which is bad news for the planet!

CO_2 is a greenhouse gas that traps the Sun's heat to keep Earth warm. The extra CO_2 from burning fossil fuels is making Earth warm up too much.

Coal makes electricity.

Coal

Fossil fuels take **350 million** years to form.

We have been using them for **300 years**.

If we keep using fossil fuels, they will last another **30-70 years**.

We won't be able to make new fossil fuels fast enough if we do use up all our supplies. That's why we call fossil fuels 'non-renewable' energy sources.

So how are we using all that energy?

GADGETS GALORE

Electrical energy travels along a network of cables to our homes, and it's amazing! Plug in a gadget or flick a switch and electrical potential energy will quickly transform into lots of other useful types of energy.

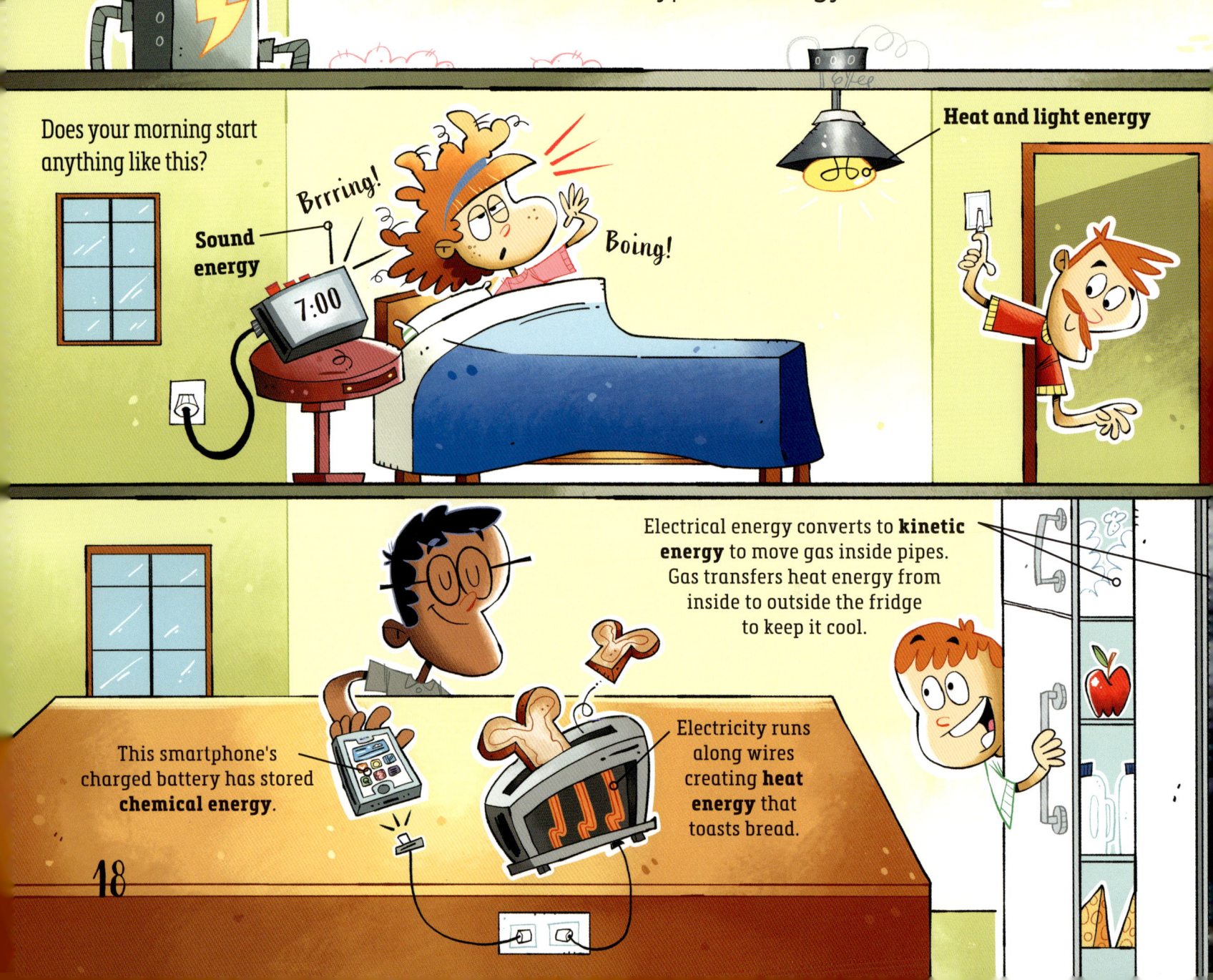

Does your morning start anything like this?

Brrring!

Sound energy

Boing!

7:00

Heat and light energy

Electrical energy converts to **kinetic energy** to move gas inside pipes. Gas transfers heat energy from inside to outside the fridge to keep it cool.

This smartphone's charged battery has stored **chemical energy**.

Electricity runs along wires creating **heat energy** that toasts bread.

18

Satellite

Stored **chemical energy** becomes **mechanical energy** when this electric car drives away.

Battery

Cold water flows over a metal element to be warmed by **heat energy**.

Did you know ...
Most gadgets don't use all the energy they suck up. Sometimes they lose heat to the area that surrounds them. Gadgets suck up energy even when you're not using them.

One per cent of world CO_2 emissions come from vampire energy.

Light, heat and sound energy

Programmes are transmitted through a signal carried by a cable, satellite or aerial.

You're wasting 'vampire' energy if your unused gadget:

• has a light on

• feels warm

• is plugged in.

If our electricity comes from fossil fuels, then using gadgets is adding CO_2 to the atmosphere. Can electricity be cleaner?

19

GOING NUCLEAR

Nuclear power produces masses of electricity and **doesn't** release CO_2.

So how does it work?

Everything on Earth is made up of all sorts of different types of atom, which are held together with energy. The centre, or nucleus, of an atom holds a huge amount of energy.

Because uranium atoms are easy to split apart, uranium is used as fuel. Splitting uranium atoms releases tiny particles that start a chain reaction creating nuclear energy.

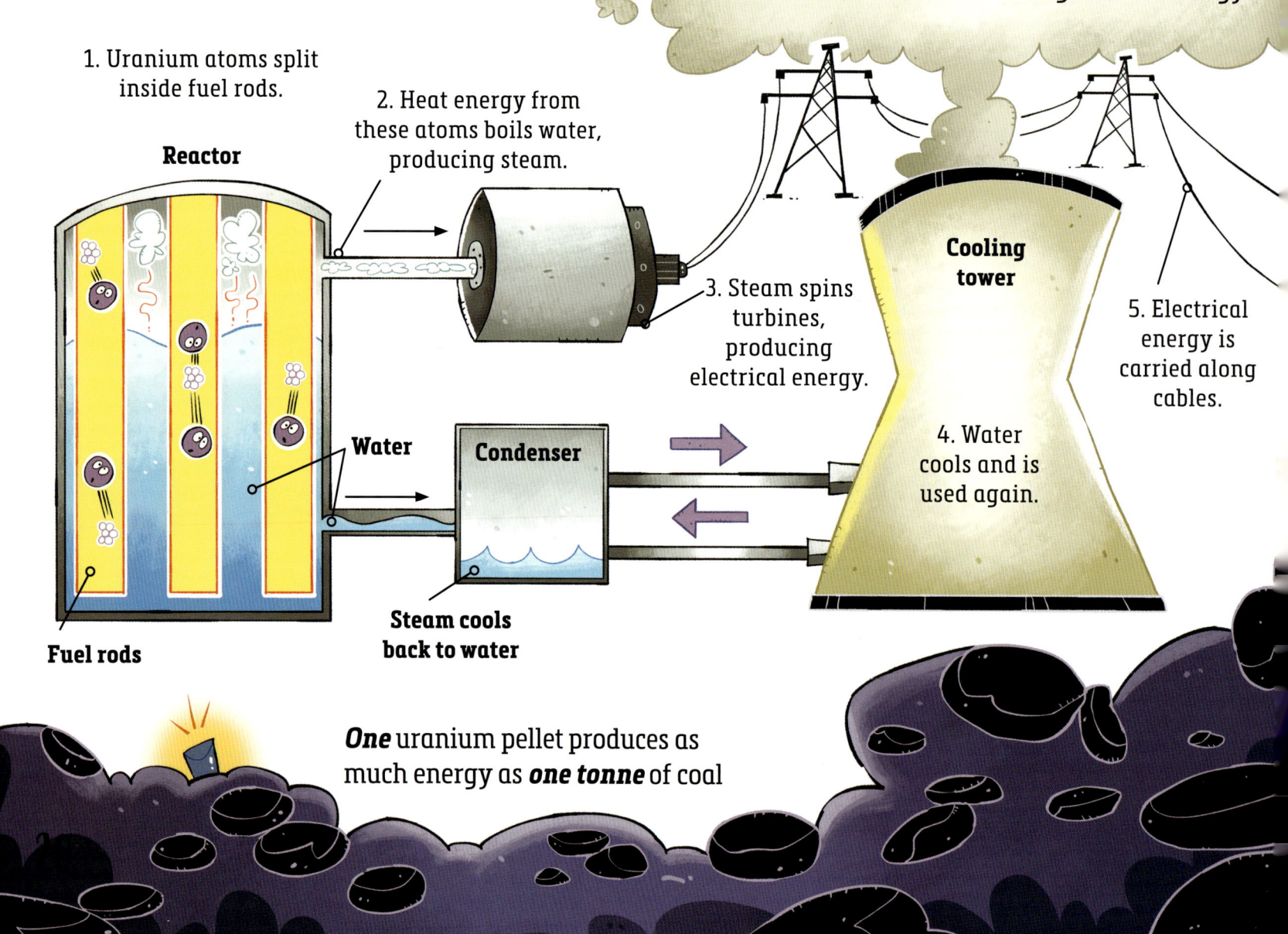

1. Uranium atoms split inside fuel rods.

Reactor

2. Heat energy from these atoms boils water, producing steam.

3. Steam spins turbines, producing electrical energy.

Cooling tower

5. Electrical energy is carried along cables.

Water

Condenser

4. Water cools and is used again.

Steam cools back to water

Fuel rods

One uranium pellet produces as much energy as **one tonne** of coal

Some people are really hot and bothered about nuclear energy...

Uranium waste is harmful!

Nuclear accidents can kill!

It causes cancer, damages the environment ...

Nuclear costs a packet!

... and has to be buried for thousands of years!

Other people argue that...

Nuclear is safer than coal!

Nuclear is cheap!

Splitting atoms doesn't produce CO_2!

Did you know ...
In 2011, an earthquake caused a giant wave to hit Japan's Fukushima Daiichi Nuclear Power Plant. The plant overheated, radiation leaked out and 47,000 people had to leave their homes.

Nuclear technology is improving and accidents are rare. It already provides 10 per cent of the world's energy. But are renewable energies a better option?

21

ALL-DAY ENERGY

The Sun beams down 5,000 times as much energy as we use on Earth each year. Because it shines every day, this 'solar' energy won't run out: it's renewable. And it's clean, because it doesn't belch out CO_2.

The Sun's light energy hits the solar panels and is converted into electrical energy.

Solar panel

How sunlight becomes energy we can use:

Solar panels are made up of smaller solar cells.

Solar cell

Electrical energy travels along wires to power the gadgets in our homes.

22

Sunshine farms

Lots of panels together make a solar farm. Bhadla Solar Park is an enormous solar farm in the scorching desert of Rajasthan, India. Rain hardly ever falls here.

There are over **10 million** solar panels at the park.

They feed energy to **1.3 million** homes.

Panels are cleaned by robots!

Solar panels aren't perfect:

- They can take up lots of space.

- They only work when the Sun shines and storing the energy they produce can be difficult.

- Making them is expensive and uses lots of energy.

Some scientific solutions include:

1. Panels on stilts let farmers plant crops beneath them. The solar panels shelter the plants from heavy rain.

3. A paste made from special proteins can be used to capture the Sun's energy (see page 10) when it is spread on to simple solar cells. These cells would be cheaper and easier to make and could be used **anywhere** in the world.

Paste for solar cell

2. Short-term batteries, like the ones in a mobile phone, can store solar energy for a few hours, so that daytime sunshine can power night-time activities.

Plant-paste panels aren't ready to use yet, so is there an answer in the wind?

CHASING THE BREEZE

Wind is air that's on the move. It's another source of energy that starts with the Sun.

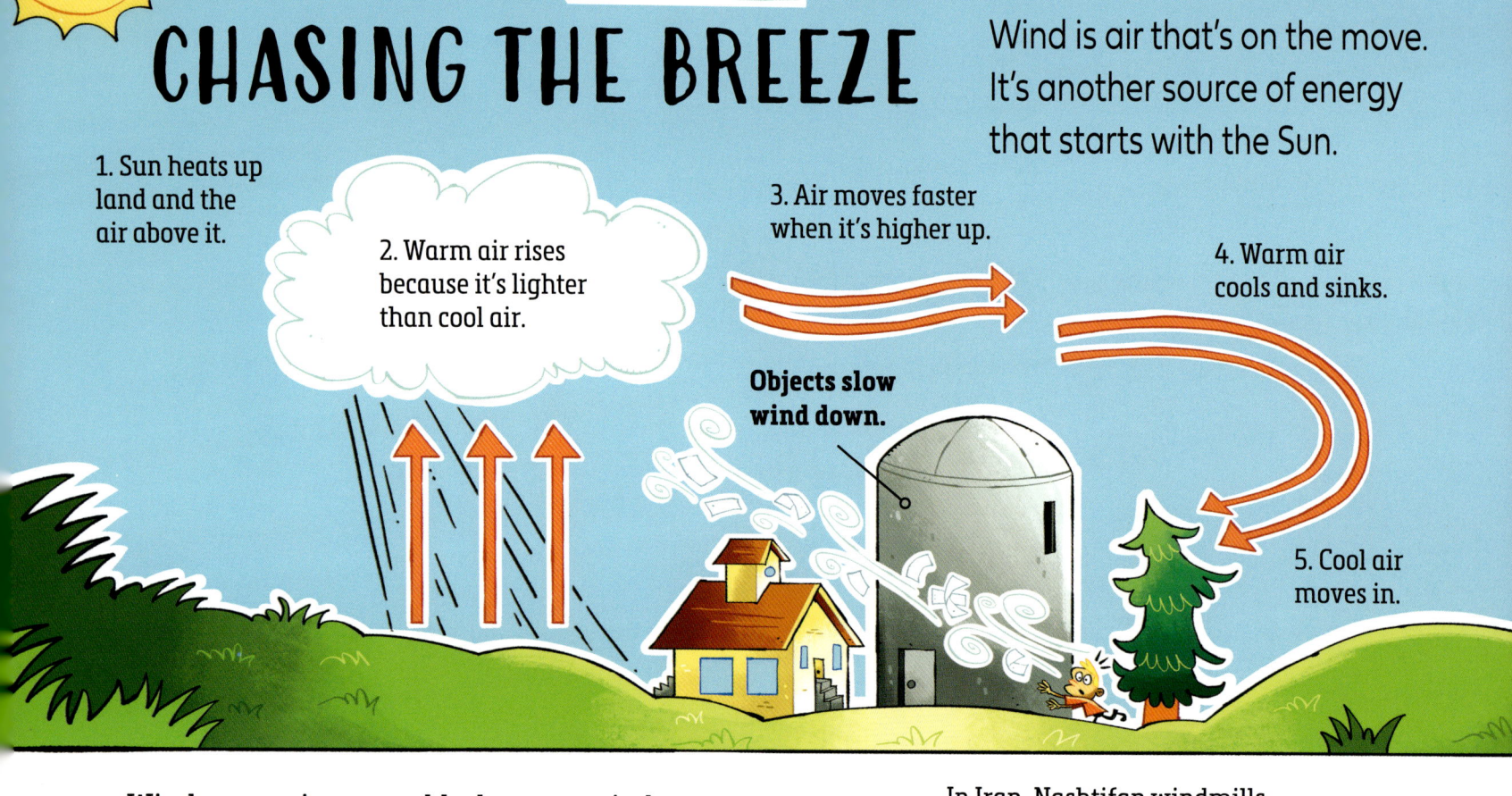

1. Sun heats up land and the air above it.

2. Warm air rises because it's lighter than cool air.

3. Air moves faster when it's higher up.

4. Warm air cools and sinks.

Objects slow wind down.

5. Cool air moves in.

Wind energy is renewable, because winds will always blow. It's clean too, because it doesn't produce CO_2.

Wind energy has been used for centuries:

In Iran, Nashtifan windmills have been grinding corn for 1,000 years.

Strong winds spin wooden blades

Blades turn grinding stone

Flour ground from wheat

In Egypt, 5,000 years ago, the wind was used to power sailing boats.

The world's first wind machine, called a turbine, was invented in 1887 by Professor James Blyth. It powered his Scottish cottage. When Blyth offered to share his invention with local villagers, they were horrified.

Cloth sails

10 m

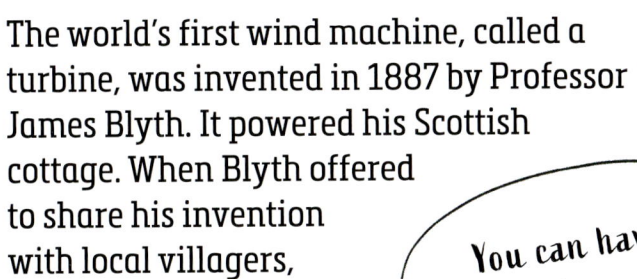

You can have one too ...

No thanks! It looks evil!

Today's turbines are much bigger and produce lots more energy.

How a wind turbine works:

Did you know ...
The tallest turbines are **280 metres** high and each one can power **20,000** homes for a year.

1. Wind sets blades spinning. This movement creates **mechanical energy**.

2. A generator and gearbox turn mechanical energy into **electrical energy**.

3. Taller towers catch faster winds.

4. Cables transport electricity.

Wind turbines are expensive to build, tricky to position and won't work if the wind doesn't blow. However, they are getting more efficient all the time.

How about using water to make energy? Would it work better?

WATER WORKS

Water energy, or hydropower, can generate a lot of electricity. Hydropower dams are often huge!

How waterpower works:

1. Reservoir holds water

2. Water turns turbines

Did you know ...
About **16 per cent** of the world's electricity comes from hydropower. It's clean, cheap (once it's built) and can work all day.

3. Turbines produce mechanical energy ...

4. ... which turns into electrical energy.

Argh! Weee!

But some people hate hydro ...

Dams can ruin river systems, destroying plant and animal habitats. Young fish that can't swim upstream are sometimes transported by truck!

Dams produce greenhouse gases from dead plants trapped in dam water.

FISH AND TRIPS

Enjoy the ride!

26

Is sea power safer?

We can capture mechanical energy from the swell of the sea when tides change. Here's the world's newest, most powerful 'tidal' turbine, the Orbital O2:

It is the size and shape of a floating jumbo jet

Yikes! What is that?

Cables carry electrical energy to users.

Turbines turn kinetic energy into electrical energy.

I'm outta here!

O2 can supply **2,000** homes with electricity.

It generates more energy than a wind turbine because more effort is needed to move water than air.

Low tide

High tide

Moon

Earth

Sun

Tidal energy is clean, renewable and doesn't need storage. It's more reliable than wind and solar. Why? Because, unlike sunshine and wind, we know when tides will happen – they follow the daily movement of Earth in relation to the Sun and Moon.

But there are more forms of renewable energy to explore ...

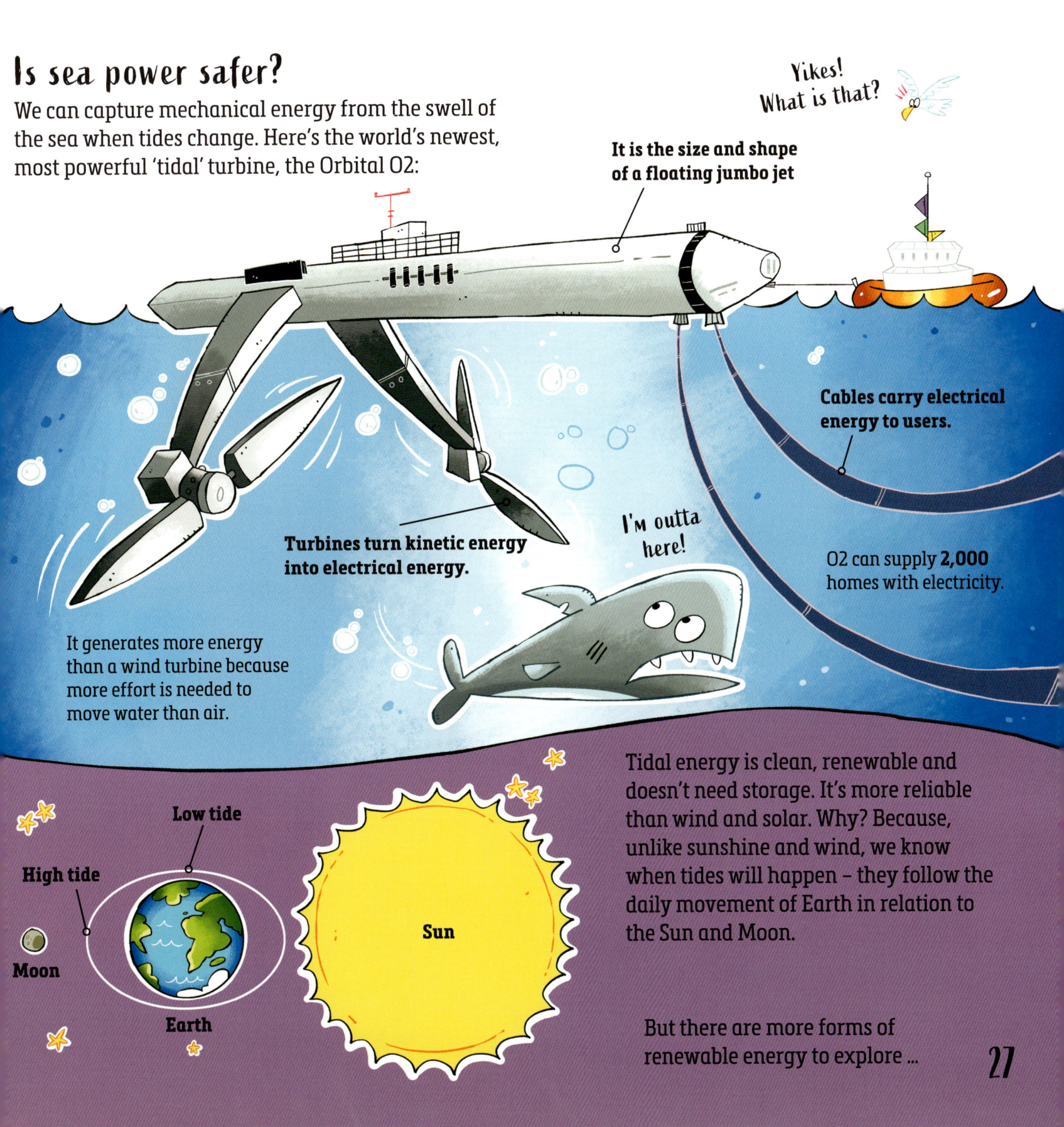

27

FAREWELL, FOSSIL FUELS

Iceland uses hydropower with geothermal energy – heat that comes from underground – to produce 100 per cent of its electricity!

Natural hot water geysers heat **90 per cent** of Iceland's homes.

Geyser

Iceland can access this underground heat because of its position on Earth.

Two of the twelve tectonic plates that make up Earth's crust meet here. So heat from inside Earth is closer to the surface.

Crust

Mantle

North American plate (left side)

Iceland

Eurasian plate (right side)

Earth's core: **6,000°C** and **3,000 km deep**

What is geothermal energy?

Heat energy changes water into steam, which turns turbines to generate electricity.

Boreholes up to 3 km deep

Hot water

Hot rock

Magma

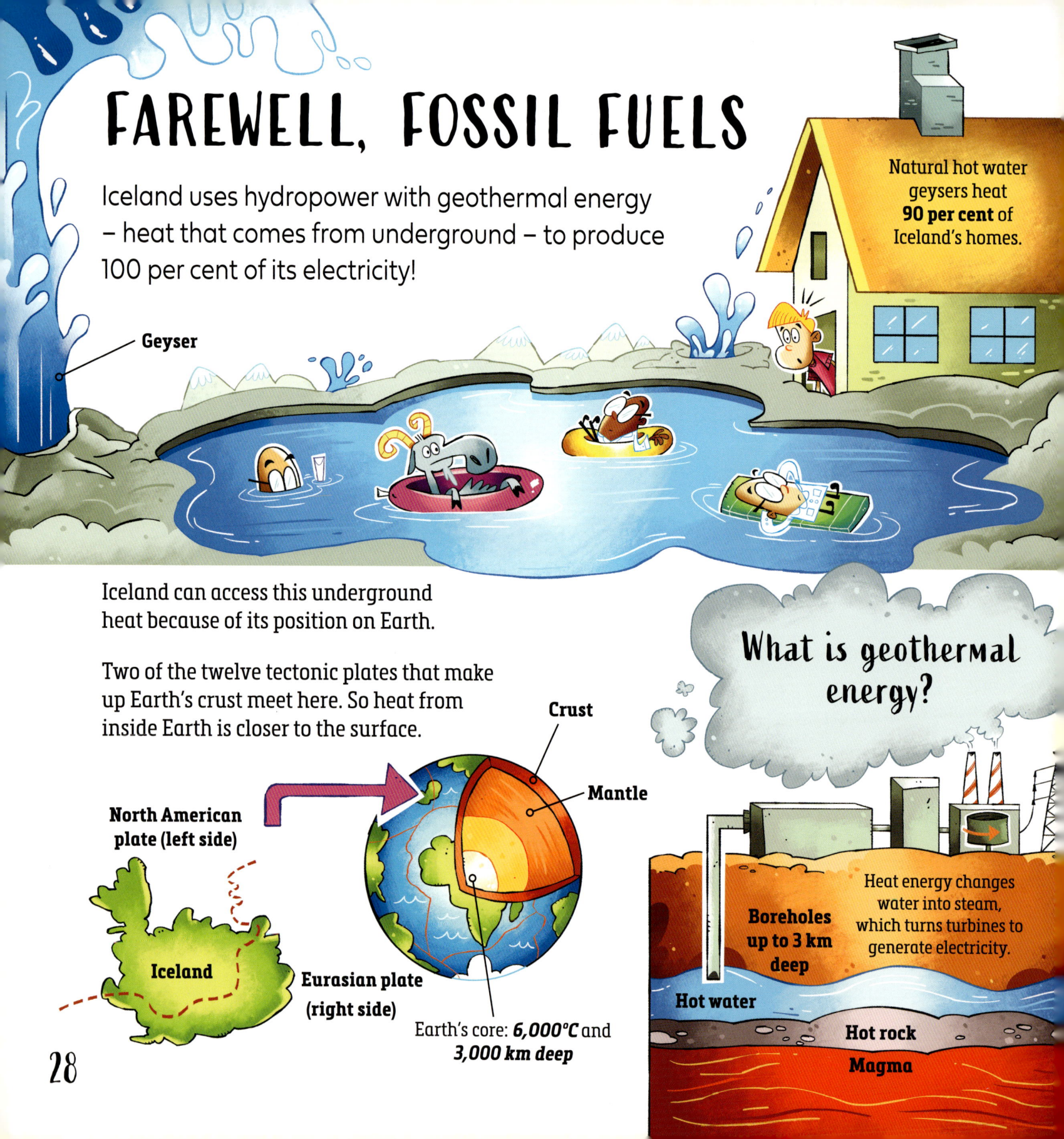

The future of energy

To protect the planet, many countries have set a target year for when they will stop using fossil fuels (see pages 16-17). Iceland's target is 2040. Most other countries are aiming for 2050 or later.

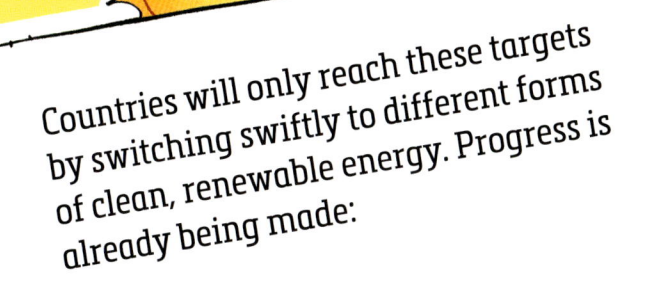

Countries will only reach these targets by switching swiftly to different forms of clean, renewable energy. Progress is already being made:

 China is building a wind farm big enough to power **13 million homes.** It will become the largest wind farm in the world.

 Indonesia is developing geothermal energy, with the help of Icelandic experts.

 Wind and solar provide **10 per cent** of the world's electricity, and that figure will keep rising.

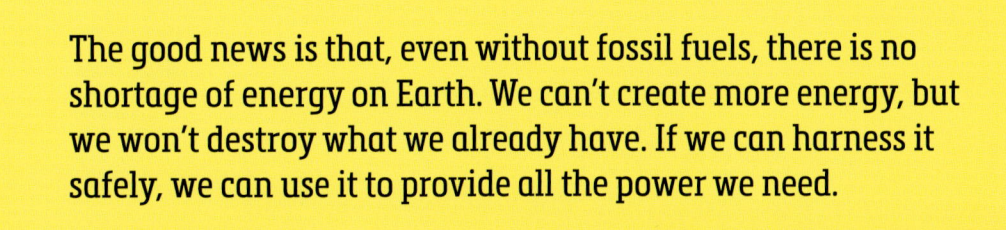

The good news is that, even without fossil fuels, there is no shortage of energy on Earth. We can't create more energy, but we won't destroy what we already have. If we can harness it safely, we can use it to provide all the power we need.

GLOSSARY

aerial – a metal rod that receives signals, e.g. to receive a radio programme

architect – someone who designs and plans the building of structures

atmosphere – the gases that surround Earth

atoms – tiny particles that stick together to make everything on Earth

carbon dioxide (CO_2) – one of the greenhouse gases that protect the planet from the sun's heat. Too much carbon dioxide (as well as other gases) in the atmosphere is trapping heat and warming the planet

chain reaction – a series of events, or reactions, each one triggered by the previous event or reaction

current – air or water moving in a specific direction; a flow of electricity

electron – tiny particles of matter that have a negative charge (see negative charge)

evaporate – when a liquid turns into a gas

force – forces, such as gravity, push or pull an object in a certain direction

fossil fuel – e.g. coal, oil or gas. Fuels produced from what's left of plants and animals that died millions of years ago

generate/generator – to produce power/a machine that produces electricity

geyser – a jet of steam that shoots up through a natural hole in Earth's surface

greenhouse gas – CO_2 and other gases that trap the Sun's heat to keep Earth warm

habitat – where an animal or plant naturally lives

harness – to control something so that it can be used

hydropower – electricity generated using the power of water

kinetic energy – the energy something has when it is moving

magma – liquid rock inside Earth

molecule – a molecule occurs when two or more atoms join together

negative charge – electrons. When an atom has more electrons than protons (positive charge) it has a negative charge

particle – a tiny piece of matter

plankton – tiny animal (zooplankton) or plant life (phytoplankton) that are eaten by other sea creatures. Phytoplankton survive through photosynthesis (see page 10)

positive charge – protons. When an atom has more protons than electrons (negative charge) it has a positive charge

potential energy – the energy something has because of its position, electric charge, etc, when it is not moving

radiation – objects that give off a lot of radiation are called radioactive. Radioactive objects can hold a lot of energy, and this can be dangerous

renewable energy – a natural type of energy, such as wind or solar, that does not damage the atmosphere and will never be used up

reservoir – a large lake or tank that stores and supplies water

transform – to change, e.g. from one type of energy to another

transmit – to send, e.g. a TV programme

turbine – a machine containing a wheel that produces power through heat energy

upstream – moving against the flow of a river, towards its source

uranium – a type of metal found in rock that can be split apart and used as nuclear fuel

FURTHER INFORMATION

Books

Alternative Energy (series) by Louise Kay Stewart (Wayland, 2023)

Building the World: Power Stations and Electricity by Paul Mason (Wayland, 2020)

A Question of Science: Where does lightning come from? by Anna Claybourne (Wayland, 2021)

Earth's Amazing Cycles: Energy by Jillian Powell (Franklin Watts, 2022)

Be a Scientist: Investigating Electricity by Jacqui Bailey (Wayland, 2020)

Videos to watch

Find out the difference between potential and kinetic energy:
youtu.be/quxEz2qxo9s

Take a closer look at geothermal energy in Iceland:
thekidshouldseethis.com/post/geothermal-energy-iceland

Explore how the brain works:
youtu.be/mFuHKJqpxPw

Websites

More lightning facts and pictures:
kids.nationalgeographic.com/science/article/lightning-

Lots of information on how the body uses fuel for energy:
www.bbc.co.uk/bitesize/topics/zjr8mp3/articles/ztfcvwx

More about fossil fuels and renewable energy:
www.bbc.co.uk/bitesize/topics/zshp34j/articles/zntxgwx

INDEX